Towards Women's Rights Protection

Towards Women's Rights Protection

By
Trilok Singh

CYBER TECH PUBLICATIONS
4264/3, Ansari Road, Daryaganj, New Delhi-110002 (India)
Ph.: 011-23244078. Fax: 011-23280028
E-Mail: cyberpublicationsdelhi@yahoo.com

Towards Women's Rights Protection

Trilok Singh

First Edition 2011

Published by G.S. Rawat
For Cyber Tech Publications
4264/3, Ansari Road, Daryaganj, New Delhi-110002
Ph.: 011-23244078, 43559448 Fax: 011-23280028
E-Mail: cyberpublicationsdelhi@yahoo.com
E-mail: cybertechpublications@gmail.com
Website: www.cybertechpublications.com

Printed at
Asian offset printers.

Contents

Preface

> "Generosity during life is a very different thing from generosity in the hour of death; one proceeds from genuine liberality and benevolence, the other from pride or fear."
>
> —*Horace Mann*

Women, in true sense is the progenator of human race. But she is not treated on par with men. No doubt, many women have made their presence on different fora, yet discrimination and crime against women are increasing day-by-day. Many statutes are enacted to curb these evil practices yet the condition of women has not improved as yet.

The present book compiles vital information on crime against women and various laws for protection of women's rights. Every care is taken to reproduce the authentic text of statutes. The following chapters make core of the study—Introduction; Crime Against Women; Marital Violence; Protective Laws for Women: An Appraisal; Optional Protocol to the Convention on the Elimination of Discrimination against Women (2000); Declaration on the Elimination of Violence against Women (1993); Convention on the Elimination of All Forms of Discrimination against Women (1981); The National Commission for Women Act (1990); The Commission of SATI (Prevention) Act (1987); The Muslim Women (Protection of Rights on Divorce) Act (1986); Protocol Against the Smuggling of Migrants by Land, Sea and Air, Supplementing the United Nations Convention

Against Transnational Crime (2004); Inter-American Convention on the Prevention, Punishment and Eradication of Violence Against Women (1995); Declaration on the Protection of Women and Children in Emergency and Armed Conflict (1974); The Women 's and Children's Institutions (Licensing) Act (1956); Inter-American Convention on the Granting of Civil Rights to Women (1949); Appendices & Bibliography etc.

Definitely, this will delight and enlighten researchers, teachers, social scientists, policy planners and social and women activists besides NGOs and voluntary organizations operating in the field.

In course of furnishing authentic information, we have consulted a number of sources—both primary and secondary, and subscribed them by way of citation or substantial reproduction. I am deeply beholden to all the experts in the field whose views/works are made use of in this work. I am equally grateful to their publishers and copyright holders. Efforts are made to acknowledge them in references and bibliography.

Simultaneously I was much benefited by inspiration, guidance and assistance of my seniors, colleagues and friends. Besides these librarieans and other staff at different libraries has extended their cooperation by making available the requisite reading materials at their helms. I am thankful to them also.

Finally, I express my gratitude to my publishers for evincing keen interest in this project and also bringing out this on shortest possible time.

—Author

1

Introduction

> "Instead of saying that man is the creature of circumstance, it would be nearer the mark to say that man is the architect of circumstance. From the same material one man builds palaces, another hovels; one warehouses, another villas; bricks and mortar are mortar and bricks until the architect can make them something else."
>
> —*Thomas Carlyle*

Every civil society boast of having accorded high status to women. Ancient scriptures and religious literature is cited for this. But in actual practice all societies in the world are men-dominated and women are maltreated.

Since in the present book we intend to elucidate crime against women and women's rights and national and international statutory provisions of that, first we must have a look on women in different societies the world over.

Man and woman are born equal and both play vital roles in the creation and development of their families in particular and the society in general. Woman is not only a bread distributor but she is also as bread winner. She is working shoulder to shoulder with men. The greatest contribution of the Indian women like her counterpart in other parts of the world is through home, husband and children. The middle class wives in the four major cities Bombay, Calcutta, Madras and Delhi constitute about 17 per cent of the total working class of population.

The history of the mankind reveals that the woman is and has been the foundation stone of a family in particular and the society in general. She is spiritual and direct agent of life forces and if the foundation is not properly maintained, the whole building of the human life is bound to crack down and dismember. Further, among the most wonderful mysteries of our nature is that sex, therefore, the mother who gives birth must have our reverence. The wife through whom we achieve parentage must have our reverence. Sex which governs so much of our physical life and has so much influence on our emotional and higher nature, deserves not our fear or contempt or our amused indulgence, but our reverence in the highest sense of term.

Woman has been given a position of pride in every religion. Under Christianity and Hinduism, they are respected and due importance is given to their" rights and privileges. Woman enjoyed a position of high esteem in the Rigveda period. No function of significance could be completed without her participation. In the Quran, a complete sura has been devoted for the welfare, rights and duties of women.

It has been rightly pointed out that women have been and will always be what man make them. However, no philosophical student of comparative religion can fail to observe that at the foundation of every spiritual faith stands a woman, whose sympathy blesses the work of infusing new life into humanity. A number of laws have been enacted in almost all the civilised countries to restore, maintain and project the status and position of the women. Such laws have also received international recognition.

Status of Women in Different Religions and Cultures

According to Socrates: "A woman is the greatest source of chaos and disruption in the world. She is like the Dafali tree which outwardly looks very beautiful but if sparrows eat it they die without fail." Greeks conceived that "Cure is possible for fire burn and snake bite but it is impossible to arrest woman's subtility"

In Chinese scripture women are called the "waters of woe" that wash away all good fortune. In Chinese life the woman was always regarded inferior to man and was conceded no rights what-so-ever. A woman was eternally regarded a minor, her very children not properly belonging to hor. A man could, whenever he pleased, repudiate his wife, or sell her as a concubine. After widowhood she remained the property of her husband's family and it was almost impossible for her to remarry. There was also female infanticide.

In Vedic society women could be admired and respected but only when men desired so. It was imperative on women to bear sons for fulfilment. The Vedas are full of prayers for birth of a son. There are prayer and ceremonials which seek to prevent birth of a daughter. In fact a daughter was denigrated. For instance in the *Aitareya Brahmana,* tells King Harischandra who had 100 wives but no son and who longed for a son: "The son is a boat of salvation a light in the highest heaven. A wife is a comrade, but a daughter is a misery."

Hindu women were not encouraged to seek *Moksha* (salvation) as they were considered unsuitable for formal religious training and knowledge. Women were openly denigrated. It was thought that only sinful souls were born as women. In Manusmriti the Hindu law giver Manu says: "In childhood, a woman must be subject to her father, in youth to her husband and in old age to her Son; a woman must never be independent because she is innately as impure as falschood. the lord created woman as one who is full of sensuality, wrath, dishonesty, malice and bad conduct."

In addition there existed the inhuman practice of *Sati* (burning of widows) and the cruel *Devadasi* system (temple prostitution). The Hindu marriage was indissoluble which continued even after the death of the husband. The Hindu woman had no property rights.

Buddhism taught that *Nirvana* (salvation) cannot be attained in the company of women. Therefore to a follower of Buddhism: "Women are, of all the snares which the tempter had spread for men, the most dangerous: in women are embodied all the powers of infatuation which blind the men of the world." Also "unfathomably deep, like a fish's course in the water, is the character of woman, robed with many artifices, with whom truth is hard to find, to whom a lie is like the truth and the truth is like a lie."

According to Hebrew scriptures, the woman is under an eternal divine curse: "Of the woman came the beginning of sin and through her we all die." The Hebrew maiden even in her father's house, stood in the position of a servant. Her father could sell her if she was a minor. In case of his death, the sons could dispose off her at their will and pleasure. The daughter inherited nothing except when there were no heirs.

The whole structure of Christian creed is based on the doctrine of original sin for which Christianity held woman responsible: "The woman whom thou gavest to be with me, she gave me of the tree and I did eat." Eve first committed the sin and caused the fall of Adam. Thus she was actually responsible for the sins of humanity.

Jesus Christ the great teacher was himself kind to women but the Christian priests treated her derogatorily. "Among all men" says St. Gregory Thaumaturgus, "I sought for chastity proper to them and I found it among none. And verily a person may find one man chaste among a thousand but among women never." According to St. Gregory of Nazianzum: "Fierce is the dragon, and cunning the asp; but woman has the malice of both." The Orthodox Greek Church denied that woman had a soul. At the Council of Macon, a bishop vehemently asserted that woman did not belong to the human species.

In the Roman Empire hot oil was poured on the bodies of women. They were dranged, tied with the tails of fast-running horses. They were tied with pillars while fire was made to approach them from the pedestals. The husband possessed the power of summarily putting the wife to death for acts like poisoning, drinking and the substitution of a spurious child.

During Middle Ages in England alone in the year 1500 C.E. a special council was set up for persecuting women. It devised new means for perpetrating cruelty and oppression on women with the result that Christians burnt nine million women alive.

Status of Women in Islam

As we have seen the condition of women before Islam was miserable throughout the world. No religion allowed them equality. No religion gave them a share in property of their parents and husbands. Woman was looked upon as an evil and an unwanted burden, a source of disgrace and humiliation for the family. Women were universally treated as chattels and their own consent in anything was considered immaterial.

In the religions of the world Islam is the only exception which gave the attribute "better half" to woman and established her separate identity, thus giving her an independent and honourable status. Islam not only dignified the status of woman but also raised it to a footing of equality with man fourteen centuries ago.

But whatever Holy Quaran syas or prescribe in actual practice women's condition in Islamic societies in critical.

2

Crime Against Women

> "Equality is not a law of nature. Nature has made no two things equal: its sovereign law is subordination and dependence."
>
> —*L.De Clapiers Vauvenagues*

It is pertinent to note that social workers, scavengers, college students, field labourers, matrons and quite brides, professionals, artists, industrialists, politicians and bureaucrats—these are all women of India. Those who have genuinely attempted to know the women of India have never been successful in finding a stereotype, because there is no single Indian woman. In fact, the diversity of women in India defies imagination. Geographic, occupational, economic, religious and caste differences are vast. But an important threat that winds through the lives of these diverse women is that of violence.

Even today, in the first decade of the 21st century, women are not being allowed to live successfully the life of a human being. Oppression, as a dramatic issue, has made headlines every where, and has received a certain degree of redress; but the endemic and frightening violence, has remained like women themselves, largely ignored.

If Sati has found a new incarnation in bride-burning,

female infanticide did not die out with the Act of 1870. The media glare may have subdued the reprehensible racket in aborting female foetuses after sex determination test under the guise of detecting cogenital abnormality—but neglect, starvation, lack of immunisation, the reluctance to 'waste' medical services on a girl, all continue to result in a slow death. This violence, whether overt or covert that begins even before birth remains in lifelong companion whether one likes it or not. In fact, life for a girl, becomes increasingly sinister, as she enters womanhood—for she could be battered or burnt within her prison like home or molested, assaulted or raped outside it.

Not surprisingly, she undergoes her metamorphosis into a woman in shame and fear. On the other hand, many kinds of masculine behaviour spring from a root of possible violence. The lack of physical power leads to a general timidity in women. She has no faith in a force she has not experienced in her body; she does not dare to be enterprising, to revolt, to invent, deemed to docility, to resignation, she can take in society only a place already made for her. History is littered with references to and formulae for, beating, clubbing and kicking women into submission, though there are some historical references to women as important, powerful, meaningful contributors to the life and times of a people.

Women's place in history has often been at the receiving end of a blow. This history is a long and sad one—sad because of the country's women who have been browbeaten, bruised, and bloodied and broken, and sad because ideologies and institutional practices that made such treatment both possible and justifiable have survived albeit somewhat altered, from century to century and been woven into the fabric of our culture and are thriving to-day. It is not possible to understand violence against women without understanding its past and the part the past plays in contemporary beliefs and behaviours.

One cannot, however, distill the essence of this violence, merely from a description of ancient practices or from the laws specifying chastisement. It requires an examination of the individual and institutional factors that reveal why women have systematically been subjected to violence.

Legal, historical, literary and religious writings all contribute to understanding the unique status of women, a status that composes the kernel of the explanation of why it is they who have become the "appropriate" victims of violence. In reality, women rarely had an identity apart from that given to them as wives, mothers and daughters and departure from that identity was discouraged and punished.

Rarely in historical or religious writings has a woman been named and discussed as an individual except in terms of an exceptional ability or inability to fulfil family obligations. Women were rarely remembered as individuals, even when they did something memorable.

They were *nameless, undifferentiated, undistinguished and indistinguishable.* They were considered to be all alike; they were merely the members of some man's family. As such, there was little or nothing the historian thought he could write about any particular one of them. Since the historian was not interested in a group of people who were seen as merely family members, they ignored women. The contradictory and unrealistic picture of what it meant to be a woman may be found in literature and history but something that was much closer to reality was reflected in laws and religion. The seeds of violence in the subordination of females lie in their subjection to male authority and control. This relationship between women and men has been institutionalised in the structure of the patriarchal family and is supported by the economic and the political institutions and by a belief system, including a religious one, that makes such relationship seem natural, morally just and sacred. Obedience, however, was something a woman could not withhold without serious consequences. It was the legal right of a man to demand obedience from a woman in the form of father, husband, brother, son, etc.

The laws specified the types of behaviour that were to be controlled, the legitimate means by which such control could be effected, and who had the right to control. In fact, the law has always seemed directed at protecting the rights and authority of men (they were the law makers, after all) and controlling and oppressing women. The structure and ideology of the patriarchal family had, of course, formed much of the basic structure and ideology of both the modern state, which emerged out and superseded that institution and the smaller less powerful nuclear family, which was encouraged by the state in order to obtain its own support and security. Thus the state and the nuclear family were inextricably interwined and mutually supportive.

The family, in fact,was the cornerstone of the patriarchal society—it was the model upon which other social institutions were based, and its order became a moral order, its hierarchy sacred.

Religious leaders placed faith in the idea that the subjection of women, which they supported so strongly, could be achieved by teaching women that it was their sacred duty to obey and by vesting men with great authority to control them. As long as the woman is not perceived as an equal human being she will continue to be relegated to the realms of violence, to be deprived and down-trodden, starved and finally defeated by the filthy lucre.

We have now recently discovered women all over again this time in a slightly more glamorous role than usual—as the "pivot of social change." But yet another role to be included in the wide repertory of order she has played through the ages. Once again an instrument, changing the face of the country-side while keeping her own hidden behind the veil of darkness. If women are to be the instrument of social change, change must begin in a less negative way.

But the fact remains that India can, at best limp into the 21st century, if our social conditioning continues to be blinkered and dehumanised by sexist bigotry. It is heartening to note that rape, battering, sexual harassment and other expressions of violence against women have begun to be confronted and responded to by women in our country, like elsewhere in the world. Women are organising in their communities, and on a national and international level to fight back and bring an end to the years of silence and abuse. The women's groups that have come forth in protest, to organise and provide services have begun a dialogue that crosses national boundaries.

The anti-rape movement, which began in India, in 1980, has gathered tremendous memontum over the past five years. Dowry deaths; police brutality and rape by Government and military representatives both against individual woman and as a tool to repress peasant movement; Sati; and rape of Dalit and Tribal women are some of the key offences that the anti rape movement has begun to address. The Mathura Rape case and the Rameeza Bee case were both well publicised cases that helped to bring national attention to the prevalence and seriousness of crimes against women. Sexual harassment on the job, child abuse and incest have yet to receive much public attention. However, these issues are increasingly getting exposure in the media and are being discussed by women's organisations. Finally, the Indian Penal Code of 1860 underwent significant changes for the first time in over 120 years with the passage of the new Rape Law of 1983.

Though the new law was both widely acclaimed and criticised by the anti-rape movement, lawyers, and the general public it has brought to the force, key issues around press censorship, age of consent, appropriate punishment, burden of proof, custodial rape, and the past sexual history of the victim.

Since male supremacy is the historical source of violence, and class domination perpetuates male privilege a long-range plan to end abuse includes a total restructuring of society that is feminist, anti-racist and socialist. While ending capitalism and building socialism will not stop male domination, they may be necessary steps in the process—argues Susan Schester.

Under capitalism private ownership creates an economy based on exploitation and a privatized family, both of which rest on female subordination. In contrast, social ownership of economic life, democratic participation in the decisions that affect one's life, and ending the separation between family and community are the hopes that a yet unrealised version of socialism offers. Material preconditions must exist to end violence against women. These conditions—shelter, adequate jobs, incomes, free health care, affordable housing, and child care—are essential to allow women independence from violent men and to enable them to live decently. Whether this is possible under capitalism, is questionable. In a privatised capitalist economy, the social purposes and value of women's work disappears; women are easily degraded, subject to the whims of men and isolated from the support of other women. Resources must be available in the form of goods, services, and jobs so that power relations between men and women in the family are equalised. A society based on a privatised, nuclear family life, separate from the community, creates unresolvable contradictions in any efforts to end violence against women in the family. If women were neither economically dependent on men nor defined as different and less, than male and female might cease to be rigid, oppositional categories in which men hold more power and are more valued. In this socialist feminist world, abuse would be defined as crime against a person.

Family life would be open for community scrutiny because the family would be part of and accountable to the community. If a false separation did not exist between the family and the community, women might lose their sense of isolation and gain a sense of entitlement to a violence, free life. In the long run, men and women together must work to define and live egalitarian sexual and social relationships in the context of a struggle to end exploitation and oppression.

Crime is a universal phenomenon and is in existence through times immemorial. In the rural environment, crimes were of a simple nature and had a low rate of incidence. It was the advent of the industrial revolution which triggered off an increase in crime as a result of urbanisation. The volume of crime shows more or less the same trend in Europe, America, Africa, Asia and Latin America. Japan is the only country where crime is on the decline.

When one glances at the crime scenario, one is made conscious of those crimes that are directed against women such as rape, dowry, immoral trafficking, kidnapping & abduction, molestation and eve teasing, indecent representation, etc.

In India like other civilised countries a number of laws have been enacted in order to provide protection to women. For instance the Dowry Prohibition Act, 1961, The Hindu Marriage Act, 1955, The Hindu Women's Right to Property Act, 1937, The Hindu Succession Act, 1956, The Dissolution of Muslim Marriage Act, 1939, The Muslim Women (protection of Rights on Divorce) Rules, 1986, The Commission of Sati (Prevention) Act, 1987, and there are various other social legislations. Moreover, there are provisions pertaining to cruelty, kidnapping, abduction and rape in the Indian Panel Code.

The laws are hardly implemented in their letter and spirit, consequently, crimes against women are on increase. "I am quite sure that our real and basic growth will only come when women have a full chance to play their part in public life. Whenever they have had this chance, they have, as a whole, done well, than the average man. Our laws are man-made, our society dominated by man, and so most of us naturally take a very lopsided view of this matter. We cannot be objective, because we have grown up in certain grooves of thought and actions But the future of India will probably depend ultimately more upon the women than the men." Gender injustice, taking the shape of crimes against women without punishment of the criminal, is escalating the world over but in India it has ancient cultural roots and modern malignant manifestations where even the guardians of social defence like the police are often found to be culprits, the dispensers of justice, like the judiciary, are allegedly biased and the legislative and executive usings, who are the operators of protective legislation, go to sleep or act perfunctorily where the victims of crime belong to the lawless gender and the masculine perpetrators are of the lawless gender. This distortion in the role justice calls for militant action and correction thro' conscientisation of the people, empowerment of women, and statutory status and punitive functions granted to social action groups and woman police.

Women in India have, notwithstanding legent and scripture, suffered for long centuries. No single religion has spared her. The social and legal culture vis-a-vis the female gender has not elevated her to an equal level, breaking with the past, insisting on egalite and making her role autonomous. Women's (Vimochana', in its semantic fullness and as a personality development project, is still distances away from her. Whatever the paramount parchment (the constitution) may intone, whatever the universal instruments may inscribe, we have miles to go and promises to keep if Gender Justice is not to be mere dope but sure hope.

Violence against women is an age old phenomenon. Women were always considered weak, vulnerable and in a position to be exploited. Violence has long been accepted as something that happens to a women. The changing social structure in India has only perpetrated violence and crime against women. Education has not brought an increase in awareness—only a shallow superiority. The dignity and solemnity and symbolic beauty of ritual is quickly being lost either in the rash of city life or in the penury of rural existence. The fact that India has often legislated for women rights before several western nations is cold comfort, when we took at how little the law is known and practised. The complexity of religions and social mores does not allow for homogenous civil rights legislations. If oppressions could be tackled by passing laws then this decade would be adjusted a golden period for Indian women when protective laws were offered on a platter. Almost every single campaign against violence on women resulted in new legislation. However some of these enactments in effect remained only on paper.

Reform of the law of provide equal rights to women, opportunity for economic independence, transformation of customs and practices which reflect the inferior social position of the women are all necessary and desirable and by themselves they might improve the status of women but are unlikely to bring them at par with men. This would happen only when the relationship between the sexes is seen as essentially complementary and non-competitive and the role of mother hood is given its due place. So far in our country only the majority community—the Hindus have benefited from social legislation improving the status of women. Polygamy and no right of divorce, which had originally placed the Hindu women in a very inferior position have been prohibited. Today the law permits only monogamy as well as divorce and both husband and wife may divorce on identical grounds. Equal rights of inheritance for boys and girls as well as giving the right of adopting to a women are some of the other charges which have benefited Hindu women. To a very large extent we can say that violence against women is part of wider current of lawlessness in society, the main cause being the Jack of respect for the law. There is no doubt that there is a rise in the crime wage against women. Rape and dowry are the two crimes that have increased greatly in recent years and this social pathology requires analysis.

Women have been subjected to various degrees of torture and exploitation through the ages, not only in India, but in other countries as well. Comparatively, women in India are better off than their counterparts in other countries in matters of social legislation, but the implementation of laws has been slow and haphazard.

Since 1960's the issue of domestic violence against women which was confined within the four walls has now become a public issue. This is because of the growing awareness amongst women of their rights and the need for protection from exploitation. Almost every single campaign against violence on women gave rise to a spate of legislation. The Constitution of India guarantees fundamental rights to all its citizens. The preamble of the Constitution resolves to secure Justice, social, economic and political, Liberty of thought, expression, belief, faith and worship. Equality of status and of opportunity and to promote among them all Fraternity assuring the dignity of the individual and the unity and integrity of the nation.

A look at the Constitution of India gives an insight into the constitutional provisions for women. The Articles relating to the Fundamental Rights of women are:

Article 14 ensures that the State shall not deny to any person equality before the law or equal protection of the laws within the territory of India.

Article 15 prohibits discrimination against any citizen on grounds of religion, race, caste, sex, place of birth, or any of them.

Article 15(3) empowers the State to make any special provision for women and children. This has resulted in legislations like Factories Act, Mines Act, etc.

Article 16(1) states that there shall be equality of

opportunity for all citizens in matters relating to employment or appointment in any office under the State.

Article 16(2) guarantees that no citizen shall on grounds only of religion, race, caste, sex, descent, place of birth, residence or any of them be ineligible for or discriminated against in respect of any employment or office under the state.

Directive principles of state policy embody the major policy goals of the welfare state. The Directive principles of State policy concerning women and having a special bearing on their status are:

Article 39 (a) which directs the State to frame its policy for ensuring that the citizens, men and women equally have the right to an adequate means of livelihood. Article 39 (d) directs the State to ensure equal pay for equal work for both men and women. Article 39 (e) directs the State to ensure that the health and strength of workers men and women are safe guarded and children of tender age are not abused and that they are not forced by economic necessity to enter avocations unsuited to their age.

Article 42 directs the State to ensure just and humane conditions of work and maternity relief.

It can be seen from the above, that the Fundamental Rights of Constitution and the Directive Principles of State Policy accord equality to women in all fields. Thus Constitutional provisions safe guard women and protect their rights from being trampled in the male dominated society.

The focus of this paper is on crimes committed against women such as rape, dowry, immoral trafficking, kidnapping, abduction, molestation, eve teasing and indecent representation, etc. and the legislation pertaining to these crimes.

Rape

Rape is the most heinous of all crimes committed against women and the damage caused due to this is irreparable. It not only ruins the life of the victimised woman, but also affects the family as a whole. It is therefore necessary to look at this crime from a broader perspective.

Rape is committed not only by the breakers of law, but also by the protectors of law. Those who are expected to protect the life and liberty of the people are themselves involved in this crime. There have been a number of cases where policemen have raped women. Gang rapes by individuals and even by policemen is well known.

The reported rape cases obtained from the National Crime Records Bureau for the years 1985 to 1989 are given below for all the States and the Union Territories. However, it is important to note that the figures given in the table represent only the number of cases which are reported, but in reality, the number is more than double. This is because a large number of cases are not reported due to the social stigma attached to it.

All these states have a high level of illiteracy, poverty and lawlessness which are some of the factors which contribute to the incidence of rape. In addition, the policing in these states is inadequate. It can also be seen that there is a steady increase in the number of rape cases reported in all the States as well as the Union Territories.

The punishment for rape depends on the person committing the rape, and also on the victim 'The minimum punishment for rape according to section 376 of the Indian

Penal Code is seven years which may extend to life and may also be with fine.

The problem, of rape is a very delicate one. No amount of police protection can actually prevent the occurrence of this crime. What is needed is a very stern action against the culprits which will act as a deterrent to prospective violators. The law and the procedures dealing with such cases need to be drastically changed.

Dowry

It is unfortunate that today even among the educated, the system of dowry reigns supreme and is deep rooted in our society. The Dowry Prohibition Act was enacted in 1961 with the objective of prohibiting the evil practice of giving and taking dowry. The Act was amended in 1984 to make the offence cognizant, to enhance the penalty (both fine and imprisonment) and to widen the scope of the Act to make it more effective. The Act was further amended in 1986 to make the penal provisions more effective and stringent. The minimum punishment for taking or abetting of dowry has been raised to 5 years with a fine of Rs 15.000/-Advertisements in newspapers, periodicals etc. offering a share of property as consideration for marriage is punishable. A new offense of Dowry Death has been included in the Indian Penal Code section 304 B. If a women is dead or the death has occured by any burns/ bodily injury other than under normal circumstances within 7 years of marriage and it is shown that she was subjected to cruelty and harassment by her husband or in-laws, such a death is called a Dowry death. Whoever commits a Dowry death shall be punished with imprisonment for a term not less than 7 years but may extend to the imprisonment for life.

It is seen that the Dowry Deaths have more than doubled from 1985 to 2010.

The Dowry Prohibition Act was a commendable step towards this evil system of dowry. In spite of all the efforts being made, dowry deaths increased. One of the methods that was sought to bring the rising number under control was by improving the property rights of the women by the Hindu Succession Act 1956 and secondly the offense against married women to be made cognizant.

It may not be out of place to mention that the evil system of dowry also leads to crimes such as female infanticide by those who cannot bear the burden of bringing up a girl child. In Bihar, there has also be a spate of forced marriages where the bridegroom is kidnapped and the wedding performed at gunpoint in order to avoid the paying of Dowry by the girls' parents.

Dowry is more a social than a legal problem. There is a need to create more awareness among the people. But at the same time, the law needs to take proper course of action against the cases reported. Efforts should be made to have special courts/tribunals to avoid delay, otherwise the very purpose of the law will be defeated.

Immoral Traffic in Women

The Suppression of Immoral Traffic in women and girls Act 1956 prohibits immoral traffic in women and girls. This was amended in 1978 and later in 1986 with the objective of making penal provisions more effective and stringent. This Act has been retitled as The Immoral Traffic (Prevention) Act 1986. The salient features are that it covers males of females who are sexually exploited for commercial purposes, enhancement of the period of imprisonment when offenses are committed against minors, appointment of trafficking police officers, interrogation of victims by women police officers or, if not, in the presence of women social workers and setting up of special courts for settling such offenses which affect women.

Statistics reveal that the largest number of cases in 1989 were reported from Tamil Nadu (7215) followed by Karnataka (2689) and Andhra Pradesh (1633). Trafficking in women and girls has become highly organised, inter-state and even international business. Flesh trade has become a flourishing business particularly in Calcutta, Bombay, and Madras, With the entry of such highly contagious diseases such as AIDS into the country, such businesses pose a series health risk to the citizens of the country since there are no proper hygiene conditions and health measures being taken.

Kidnapping and Abduction of Women and Girls

Incidence of Kidnapping and abduction cases are on the in crease. The Number of Kidnaping & Abduction cases in India according to Crimes in India published by National Crime Records Bureau (MHA).

A major objective of kidnapping and abduction other than for ransom is for the purpose of immoral trafficking in women.

Molestation and Eve-Teasing

Molestation and eve teasing have become a common feature. It may be observed that the incidence is on the rise as a result of the influence of movies. An attempt is now being made to restrict the release of such displays on the screen.

Indecent Representation of Women

Indecent Representation of Women (Prohibition) Act

was passed in 1986 with the main objective of having separate legislation to effectively prohibit the indecent representation of women through advertisements, books and pamphlets. The Indecent Representation, of Women is defined to mean the depiction of the figure of a woman in a way so as to have the effect of being indecent or of being derogatory to or likely to deprave, corrupt or ignore the public morality and to prohibit all advertisements, publications, etc., which contain indecent representation of women, in any form. Offenses under this Act are made punishable with imprisonment for a term of two years and a fine of two thousand rupees on the first conviction. In the event of the second or subsequent conviction, the punishment is not less than six months which may extend to five years and also with a fine not less than ten thousand rupees but which may extend to one lakh rupees.

It may be observed that in spite of all these measures, crime against women is increasing day by day. A women feels insecure in the male dominated world. Her only drawback is her lack of physical strength as compared to a man. In this society which is becoming more and more violent, crime against women becomes a great setback to the advancement of women. Hence the problem needs to be tackled on war footing.

There should be awareness of these crimes in society, the law-enforcement agency needs to be strengthened and women themselves should be properly equipped to defend themselves.

A prerequisite to handle crime and criminals is to improve the system of policing since effective policing which can combat crime is the need of the hour. Although it may not be possible to eradicate crime completely, efforts must be made to minimise it. The law enforcement agency must be made more effective by giving them special training and involveing more and more women in the process of investigation to deal with these crimes.

It is also found that many a time a good case is lost in judiciary for want of evidence. The judges should be made to realise that it is more of a social problem than a legal one and therefore the judicial decision can go a long way in minimising this menace.

REFERENCES

1. Ali, S.A.: *Islamic History and Culture* (1978), 52.
2. Ali, T.A., *The Meaning of the Glorious Quran,* Vol. 1, p. 78.
3. Batla, M.L. and Batla, *S.: Maintenance, Marriage and Divorce* (1978)1-5.
4. Chhabra, K.S.: 'Woman and the Law', *Law Journal of the Guru Nanak Dev University,* Vol. 10, No. 1 (Mar. 1982).
5. Iyer Krishna V.R.: 'Crime Against Women—A *Saga of Victimology Sans Penology* 'in (Ed.) Sgama O.C. *'Crime Against Women',* 1994, Ashish Publishing House, New Delhi.
6. Nayak, J.T.: 'Women and Development in India' see also Nayak; J.T. and Pinto, S.C. (eds.). *Towards Self Reliance, Income Generation far Women,* June 25, 88.
7. Mishra Suresh: *'Women, Violence and the Law'* in the edit. Book of Sharma, O.C. *'Crime Against Women'* 1994. Ashish Publishing House, New Delhi
8. Misra, S.: Dowry Deaths: *An Approach,* Vol. XXX No. 2, (Oct.-Dec. 1983) 30-34.
9. Mir Mearj-ud-din 'Crime Against Women: A Critical Analyis', Ashish Publishing House, New Delhi.
10. Negla B.K.: *'Women and Law'* Rawat Publication, Jaipur, 1991.

3

Marital Violence

"If thy daughter marry well, thou hast found a son; if not thou hast lost a daughter."

—*Francis Quarles*

Relation Between Partners in Marriage

First it is remarkable that marriage in every society is a bond that in the present society is based on the companionship. In Indian society, however, the woman enters into marriage with old values and convictions. She is expected to shift her loyalties from parents and siblings to husband and in-laws. Socially, after her marriage, she has no independent social or economic status of her own. Her social status is directly determined by and is dependent on her husband's status in the family. In some families, the husbands give equal status to their wives but in most cases, particularly in low and middle-income groups, the illiterate and less-educated and economically dependent wives are made to feel empty and meaningless.

Whenever a family runs into problems, such problems are generally alleged as caused by a single member — the wife, even though the family consists of a number of individuals. For all marital problems also, it is the wife who is criticised for maladjustment. In power relations, it is the husband who remains aggressive.

The marital violence is mostly directed by the husband against the wife. Even if the wife gets the chance of expressing her anger, relatiate to aggressive behaviour and return the insult, she prefers to tolerate victimisation and remain passive and docile. The girl's childhood training and adolescence experiences also conditions her to oppression and violence in our society.

Here are cited some case studies.

One important difficulty in analysing the problem of wife-beating is the problem of operationalising the concepts of 'wife-abuse' and 'wife-battering.' The two terms 'abuse' and 'battering' are pejorative, emotion-charged terms used to draw attention to behaviour considered deviant. These terms have been applied to the narrow issue of physically striking a member in the family and causing injury to the act of striking a person with the intent of causing harm or injury but not actually causing it, to acts of violence where there is high potential of causing injury, and to acts where there is no actual hitting at all but there are acts such as verbal abuse or emotional violence.

Because of the variation in nominal definitions of battering, there is a resulting lack of comparability among various investigations of types of wife-abuse and wife beating. Here we use the term 'wife-beating' for our research defined as 'wilfully striking wife by a husband with or without injury.' This definition is limited to acts of physical violence directed towards spouse.

Severity in Beating

Severity of violent acts in wife-beating cannot be assessed in a society like India either in terms of arrests and convictions or in terms of hospitalisation or divorces, the reasons are that however violent the beating may be, the wives generally suffer it in silence. Similarly, unless the injuries are very severe, they avoid hospitalisation. The severity of beating in our culture can be measured only in terms of: how often the wife suffered injuries or became unconscious, how many times she had left her husband's house and gone to parent's or some kin's house, and how many times did she require medical attention without hospitalisation or after being hospitalised.

If the cause of beating as given by the batterers and the battered are rearranged and given in sociological terms, it could be said that about half the beatings were the result of husband's nature and/or his superiority or inferiority complexes, one-third were the result of wife's personality traits and little less than one-fourth were the result of economic conflicts. However, the understanding of violence in husband-wife relationship needs a holistic approach and diagnosis of several causes.

These causes are to be taken as complementary to each other and as interlocking pieces of a large whole. We will discuss these factors under three heads: (i) personality traits (of batterers and victims) in beating, (ii) situational factors in beating, and (iii) social norms in beating:

(i) Personality Traits in Beating

The personality traits of batterers and victims need to be analysed separately.

Some female respondents identified some traits in their husbands which they thought gave them a typical personality. Some traits of this violence-prone personality of the batterers were: suspicious, suggestible, too sexual, dominant, irrational immoral, too easily emotionally disturbed, unjust, jealous, and possessive. These traits made the risk for battering very high.

However, we believe that traits developed due to early family life affect the aggressive behaviour of a person in adulthood. In this regard, the background factors may be examined in terms of three-sub-factors: (i) socio-economic descriptors, (ii) batterer's history of abuse as a child, and (iii) exposure to spousal violence during childhood. The first factor has already been analysed under the sub-heading "the battered and the batterers." Here the last two factors will be examined as "Early family life."

As regards the early family life, the reports of the batterers themselves and in some cases of the victims about their husbands' previous life experiences indicate that the behaviour of the batterers engaging in violent behaviour was mostly learned. Information about the batterers' Childhood, adolescence and early adulthood experiences point out that they learnt to respond to all emotionally distressing cues with angry and violent behaviour.

One measure of violence is to find out how widespread is batterer's violent behaviour. In particular, is he violent only with his partner, or with partner and children, or with all family members, or with both family members and persons outside the home.

The attribution of marital violence to background factors refers to Generational theory which points that growing up in a violent home increases the likehood that an individual will be violent as an adult, both to spouse and children.

Taking the complete data together we can say, our data support the "Social Learning" theory of violence, where early socialisation to violence teaches reinforces violence as a method of conflict resolution or as a coping mechanism.

Moreover, we assume that several factors encourage discriminative spouse care, such as illicit relations with some women, nagging nature of wife, wife's chronic illness, wife paying more attention to her own parents and sibling, and neglecting husband's family members, and so forth. It follows that sullen, gloomy and unforgiving husbands will find it more difficult to develop deep affection for their spouses. No wonder, our study also revealed that of those 64 battering husbands whom we could interview, only 51.6 per cent admitted having 'partner feeling' towards their spouses. Such data suggests that the risk of wife-beating would be greater for unattached and uncommitted husbands than attached and committed husbands.

(ii) Situational Factors in Beating

The degree and nature of wife beating may be affected by stressful situations in the family, like poverty, unemployment, conflict between mother-in-law and daughter-in-law, and so forth.

Poverty provides an economic environment with insufficient discretionary resources to generate conflicts in family leading to wife-abuse.

It is not clear whether alcohol induces violent behaviour directly or whether it acts primarily as a disinhibitor of pre-existing aggressive tendencies. The latter hypothesis is perhaps supported by the notion (Blumer, 1973) that some perpetrators drink for courage prior to beating wives (or committing crimes against persons). But not a single case was reported to us in which the batterer became intoxicated for the specific purpose of assaulting his wife. But we cannot provide any proof that alcohol intake alone elicits violent behaviour.

There are many people who take alcohol yet they do not indulge in wife-beating. The use of alcohol in wife-beating may, therefore, be accepted as a 'co-operative' factor rather than the 'basic' or 'chief factor.

(iii) Social Norms in Beating

Finally, we come to the role of social norms in wife beating. Violence against wives grows out of the nature of society itself. As already mentioned social norms in our society justify male violence against women. These norms are dominant not only in lower class but also in middle and upper classes. These norms are indicated more in the process of marital adjustment and maladjustment.

Marital maladjustment can be described as the main cause of wife-beating. This maladjustment may arise both because of the personality characteristics of husbands and wives as well as environment in which their marriages function.

Adjustment of a daughter-in-law with her mother-in-law, particularly of a working daughter-in-law, is most difficult. Mother-in-law who are non-working and under complete dominance of their husbands feel jealous of and frustrated at the sudden independence and freedom of their daughters-in-law. This is countered by poisoning the ears of their sons and antagonising them against their wives.

The way Indian sons are socialised, they give more importance to their mother's briefing than their wife's protests. The poor wife is always told that it is her fault, and fault may mean anything — from cooking unwanted dishes to keeping house untidy and talking 'loudly' with the in-laws. The husband's liking is the last liking. If he dislikes, he has a 'right' to beat her and set her right.

Implicit, is the belief that if the wife does not behave, her punishment is beating.

Who are the women who suffer beating by husband in silence? On the basis of the above analysis we could say, women who suffer battering in silence are those:

- Who consider marriage as sacrament not admitting any outside interferance.
- Who are completely dependent on their husbands for economic, emotional and social support.
- Who do not approve divorce due to its social consequences, and
- Who are masochists, i.e., who got satisfaction from self-inflicted pain and humiliation.

To conclude, we can say that our data indicate that events which occurred in childhood as well as events which occurred in husband-wife relationship contribute much to violence against wife. Our data also leads us to conclude that there are some personality traits which would suggest a violence prone personality for women, just as there is indentifiable violence-prone personality for men.

The high-risk category of women for beating are: women who are traditional submissive, unintelligent and irrational, who lack confidence in self and who have weak ego and low self-esteem. On the other hand, the high-risk category of abusers are those men who have very conservative attitudes toward women, who have uncontrolled jealousy, who had faced battering in childhood, who are depressed and insecure and suffer from status frustrations, and who are always afraid of and worried about losing their influence and control over women's lives.

We, however, admit that some of these characteristics leading to battering as identified by us are based on inferences from the analysis of relationships and not on scientific measurements through the use of scales. For example, we could not measure women's low self-esteem and weak ego and offender's depression due to lack of training in psychology and due to the fact that our research was not designed to test this type of formulation.

In spite of identifying the personality traits in high-risk categories of victims and batterers, we cannot predict marital violence because besides the role of personality characteristics, there is the role of situation too, as we have already mentioned. Besides, the precipitating factor in the situation is very crucial. Thus, explanation of marital violence must incorporate situational or contextual as well as an assessment of the personality traits of both victims and assaulters. Thus, wife battering may be attributed more to the failings of the individual members rather than to the structure of the family.

Theoretical Perceptions

Do battered wives play any role in battering? Are those wives who are beaten by their husbands different from those who are not beaten? In comparing victims with non-victims, there is the assumption that the difference in the two categories exists. Though we did not study non-victims but we may refer here to four theoretical approaches which have been mainly used in analysing wife's role in battering: (i) traditional sex-role socialisation approach, (ii) 'provocative wife' argument approach. Let us first understand these approaches before giving our own analysis of the victims's background.

(i) Traditional Socialisation Approach

This approach has been used by Martin Moore, Pagelow and Walker. In this approach, wives are seen as playing an important role in beating because they are traditional. They do not change and they think the situation is inescapable. They believe men have a right to beat women, or it is women's fault if men beat them, or women have no right to protest. They do not let their husbands know that enough is enough. They believe all this because they mindlessly accept the traditional 'sex-role ideology' delivered by the socialisation process. Possibly their traditional views were nurtured by their families.

(ii) Provocative-wife Approach

This approach has been used by Gayford and Gelles. According to this approach, wife is beaten by her husband because she asks for it, or when victim contributes to it (beating) through her provoking actions. This approach thus believes in 'victim-precipitated violence' as different from 'non-victim precipitated violence'

Some women are so arrogant, haughty, uncompromising and intolerant, and make the husband's life so miserable through calculated acts of social misconduct that even the most reasonable man would lose control of himself after a certain stage and beat up the erring woman.

The believers in this approach suggest that if researchers rate men on 'frustration tolerance' and women on 'provocation potential,' the outcome would be that "if men with high frustration tolerance are paired with women of high provocation, violence is not likely to arise; but women of high provocation with men of low frustration would produce a combination where violence could be predicted.

(iii) Learned Helplessness Approach

This approach has been used by Ball and Wyman and Walker. According to this approach, some events occur in the battered women's life from childhood with sufficient regularity because of which they acquire feelings of helplessness and poor self-images and believe that they cannot escape the abuse and they only have themselves to blame. Some important events in women's early lives which suggest a susceptibility factor include a high level of violence by members in the childhood families (e.g. battered by mother, battered by father, father battered mother, father-mother, battered other children), perception of critical or uncontrollable events in childhood, and experiencing such conditions which place them at high risk for depression. The fear of losing husband's affection and the fear of disruption of their home life status-quo also prompts them to tolerate husband's battering. The battered wives are thus afraid to stay and terrified to leave for fear of inescapable reprisals.

(iv) Personal Resource Approach

This approach has been used by Bowker, Goode, O'Brien, and Rounsaville. According to this approach, battering is common in those families in which the husband doesn't possess the superior skills, talents or resources and he isn't man enough to rule the roost in the normal way. Because of his deficiencies, his wife outshines his as a result of which he hits her to become the boss again.

Let us now examine to what extent our data shows that battered women are traditionalists, or their battering is the result of their own provocation, or it is the result of their learned helplessness, or it is due to lack of personal resource factors.

(a) Victim's Attitudes and Socialisation

Why do battered women do not terminate their marriage legally or desert their partners? When asked whether the victims knew that there is a legal way to and marriage, almost all admitted having such knowledge.

However, we cannot say, how far victims' traditional beliefs were the causes of their battering. This is because we did not study the traditional women who are not battered; not we studied the 'modern' women (i.e. wives who don't take shit) who are battered/not battered, nor the variations in husbands' and wive's beliefs. It is, therefore difficult to say as to what extent beating is caused by the traditional beliefs and attitudes or childhood socialisation patterns of the battered wives, or whether traditional sex-role socialisation has any bearing on wife-beating.

(b) Victim's Provocation

Like 'socialisation' approach, 'provocation' approach also assumes wifely culpability. But the word 'provocation' as analysed by us here means that it is the wife who decides what she thinks with provoke her husband or what she considers as her 'guilt.' There may be some characteristics which wife may consider 'bad' as perceived by her but these may not be perceived as 'irritants' by her husband. 'Silence' can be aggravating but it can have a soothing effect too. Thus, operational definition of 'provocation' depends either on husband or on wife than on the researcher. Since the same characteristic may be considered provocation by one husband or wife but not by other husband or wife, it is difficult to hold as to what extent 'provocation' approach explains battering by husband. Wife's role cannot be evaluated in terms of wife's own self-aggrandizing version.

(c) Victim's Learned Helplessness

It signifies their pragmatism and rationality and may be lack of alternatives. It is possible that some victims overlook some alternatives open to them due to their sports sightedness or erroneous judgements ambiguous situations. It will be, therefore, invalid to assume that women's battering is the result of their own learned helplessness and characterological disorder.

(d) Inadequate Resource Base

In addition to the 'partner' feeling, we also believe that an "inadequate resource base" of the wife also decreases her potentiality to face her husband's beating. As already described earlier, wife-beating is found more in lower and middle classes and illiterate or less educated homes.

Knowing that in Indian society, women are discriminated in employment, promotions, and pay, etc., it would be difficult to find many of the purportedly wife-dominant or wife-superior families which supposedly drive husbands berserk. We, therefore, cannot accept (husband's inadequate) personal resources theory to explain wife beating.

Besides the above-mentioned four theoretical approaches used by western scholars to explain wife battering as already discussed in the preceding pages (namely, traditional sex-role socialisation theory provocative behaviour theory, learned helplessness theory, and personal resource theory, three other theories have also been proposed. These are: coercive theory, behavioural cyclical theory and status inferiority theory.

William Coode has maintained that husbands used physical force or its threat against wives because violence is crucial to the maintenance of family. Thus, according to him, use of physical force is an integral part of the institution of family and is one of the means to maintain control in the family. He argues, it force does not exist, the structure of the family system would be destroyed. In fact, Goode has used this thesis of use of violence between all members in the family, e.g., parents against children, parents-in-law against daughters-in-law, and even wife against husband.

But Goode's analysis is hinged on an abstracted conceptual model (exchange theory). He forgets that family roles and restrictions are backed not by force and physical restrictions alone but also by love and affection and concepts of moral responsibility and social duty. Walker's Cyclical Theory of violence maintains that interaction between husband and wife tends to follow a cyclical pattern, alternating between hostility and love. He says that three phases occur in a cycle in battering relationships. First is the phase of tension-building and third is the phase of loving contribution, i.e. phase characterised by an absence of tension or violence. In between, we have the second phase.

Over time, the first phase becomes more common and the third phase declines.

Status inferiority theory maintains that the rate of wife beating is greater when the wife has a more prestigious job than her husband. This theory is thus not much different from the Personal Resource Theory we have already analysed in the preceding pages. Our reaction to these theories is like the four theories discussed earlier, i.e., these three theories also fail in explaining wife battering. Walker's Cyclical Theory does not hold good because it is difficult to find any phase in which there is no conflict between husband and wife or there is complete harmony between the two. Further, conflict and harmony are continuous phenomena; they do not appear in Cyclical order.

Status Inferiority Theory cannot be accepted as now which explains wife battering because situations in which wife has higher status than her husband are rare in our society. We did come across some cases where wife earned more than her husband; but it is not the 'earnings' that determine husband-wife relationship in our society; rather it is the traditional attitude of wife towards husband which forces her to accept husband's dominance and authority, whatever be his income or educational level.

The Recent Approaches

Two approaches used in 1980 in explaining violence against women been described as important contributions in the field of sociology of 'Violence.' One is 'Feminist approach' used by Dobash and Dobash (1980) and other is 'Balance of Power' approach used by Straus, Gelles and Steinmetz (1980). The former attempts to establish a link between patriarchy as a social system and violence against women, while the latter focuses on interpersonal power relations and husband's dominance in analysing women's abuse.

The central argument of Feminist approach is that the brutalisation of an individual woman (particularly in the family) by an individual man is not an individual or family problem. It is simply one menifestation of the system of male domination of women which has existed historically and cross-culturally. Societal tolerance of woman's abuse, including wife beating, is a reflection of partiarchal norms which support male dominance in marriage. Unless new norms of marriage and family are created, women will continue to be abused and ill-treated because of time-honoured traditions. In this context, Dobash and Dobash assert that men who assault women are actually living upto cultural prescriptions that are cherished in society-aggressiveness, male dominance and female subordination — and they are using physical force as a means to enforce that dominance. Thus, they believe that the problem (violence against women) lies in the domination of women and the answer lies in the struggle against it.

The question is: do we have empirical evidence regarding the impact of sexual inequality? Without the quantitative data, how could this explanation be described as logical and rational?

The Marital Power approach is based on marital relationships and marital interaction. It focuses not on structured inequality on the societal level but on inequality and the balance of power within the family. Straus in his study (1980) found that the level of violence against wives is lowest among couples who folled a pattern of egalitarian decision-making. Clearly, husband violence is associated with non-egalitarian decision-making.

While this study provides valuable evidence on the relationship between husband dominance and violence, it is too narrowly focused. It explains only wife-battering and the consequences of inequality within the confines of the family unit. We want a general explanation to analyse varied types of violence against women.

REFERENCES

1. Ahuja, Ram, *Crime Against Women*, Jaipur: Rawat Publishers, 1986.

2. Alfaro, J., (1978, Child Abuse and Subsequent Delinquent Behaviour, New York.
3. Ball, P.G. and Wyman, "Battered Wives and Powerlessness," in *Victimology,* 1977-78, pp. 325-534.
4. Bandura, A. (1973). *Aggression: A Social Learning Analysis,* Englewood Cliffs: Prentice Hall.
5. Blumer, D., "Neuropsychiatric Aspects of Violent Behaviour," Proceedings of the National Symposium of Medical Sciences and the Criminal Law, Centre of Criminology, University of Toronto, Canada, pp. 73-87.
6. Bowker, L.H., "Wife beating" in Women and Crime in America, New York: Macmillan, 1981.
7. Fagan, Jeffrey, A.; Stewart Douglas, K.; and Hasen Karen, V., (1983). "Violent Men or Violent Husbands," in *The Darkside of Families* ed. by Finkelhor, Gelles, Hotaling and Strauss, Beverly Hills: Sage Publications, pp. 49-67.
8. Gayford, J.J., "Battered Wives" in Martin, J.P. (ed.), Violence and the Family, England: John Wiley, 1978.
9. Gayford, J.J., "Battered Wives" in Violence and the Family, ed by J.P. Martin, England: John Wiley, 1978, p. 33.
10. Gelles, R.J., *The Violent Home,* Beverly Hills: Sage Publications, 1972.
11. Goode, W.J., "Force and Violence in the Family," in Steinmetz and Strauss (ed.), *Violence in the Family,* New York: Harper and Row, 1974.
12. Hilberman, E. and Munson, M. "Sixty Battered Women," *Victimology,* An International Journal, 1977-78, pp. 460-471. Quoted by Woldfgang and Weiner "Criminal Violence," *op. cit.*
13. Martin, D., "What keeps a woman captive in a violent relationship," in Moore, D.M. (ed.) *Battered Women,* Beverly Hills: Sage Publications, 1979.
14. Moore, D.M. (ed.) Battered Women, Beverly Hills: Sage Publications, 1979.
15. O'Brien, J.E., "Violence in Divorce-prone Families," in *Journal of Marriage and Family,* 1971, pp. 692-698.
16. Pagelow, M.D. in Bowker, L.H. (ed.), *Women and Crime in*

America, New York: Macmillan, 1981.

17. Potts, D.A.; Herzberger, S.D.; and Holland, A.E., (1979). "Child Abuse," quoted by Richard Gelles in Domestic Criminal Violence in Woldfgang and Weiner, *Criminal Violence, op. cit.,* pp. 201-230.
18. Rounsaville, "Theory in Marital Violence," In *Victimology,* 1978, pp. 11-31.
19. Scrells, J.M. (Jr.), (1977), "Kids who Kill," in *Crime and Delinquency.*
20. Tinklenberg, J.R., "Alcohol and Violence," in Bourne and Fox (eds.), *Alcoholism Progress in Research and Treatment,* New York: Academic Press, 1973.
21. Walker, L., *The Battered Women,* New York: Harper and Row, 1979.
22. Walker, L.F., "Battered Women and Learned Helplessness", in *Victimology,* 1977-78, pp. 325-534.
23. Wolfgang, M.E., "Violence in the Family," in Kutash *et al. Perspectives in Murder and Aggression,* San Francisco, 1978.

4

Protective Laws for Women: An Appraisal

Crime against women in increasing day by day. The empirical survey of crimes against women brought into focus the pathetic condition of law enforcement agencies and the ineffectiveness of the protective laws to curb the growing incidents of crimes against women. Comprehensive survey of the general crime scene revealed that the publication of the Report of the Committee on the Status of Women in 1974, the celebration of the Women's Decade (1974 to 1984) on a global scale and the exposure by the media of innumerable cases of crimes against women specially the growing incidents of heinous crimes like bride burning and rape in 1970s and the negligible rate of conviction and jolted the academicians, law-makers and women's organisations out of their escapist reverits.

It had forced them to re-examine the laws on crime against women and to find out the reasons of the failure of protective legislation. It also compelled them to think more seriously about this socio-legal problem and to devise better ways of combating this evil.

Legal Activity

A Law Commission was appointed with the task of reexamining the laws and to suggest measures for making them more effective. A Select Committee of Parliament was formed to scrutinize the suggestions from women's organisations and other enlightened sections of the society. As a result of these efforts many new laws were passed and old ones were amended.

The Dowry Prohibition Act, 1961 was amended in 1983 and changes were again made in 1986 to make it more dynamic. Massive changes were made in IPC and Cr. PC. The Common Law principle of the innocence of the accused was done away with in cases of custodial rape, cruelty towards the wife and dowry deaths. In early eighties dowry became a pejorative term, fanning animus against it were the women's groups. Young boys and girls took oath not to seek dowry and refuse to marry if dowry was demanded. But it was a very short lived euphoria and died down very fast.

In 1986 Immoral Traffic (Prevention) Act was passed, it replaced SITA of 1956. Several changes were made in the Evidence Act to facilitate the proof of cases connected with dowry deaths and custodial rapes. Delhi Eve Teasing Act, 1988 was passed to curb the increasing incidents of eve teasing.

Remarkably, special cell, Crimes (Women) Cell was established in 1983 to combat the growing incidents of cruelty, wife beating, harassment and torture of women. A number of Women's Organisations were given statutory recognition to help the oppressed women fight for their rights. In 1984, Family Court Act was passed to expedite cases related to family matters.

A Perspective Plan for women was conceived of and several Commissions on women like the Self Employed

Women's Commission, Commission on Women in Custody, and National Commission of Women were appointed. In 1989 an All India Conference on Nyaya Panchayats was held and a Conference of Law Ministers was held in 1991 to consider the proposals put forward by the Malimath Committee on Arrears.

A conference of Chief Justices of High Courts was held in September 1992 to consider the possibility of adopting a code of conduct for the judges. All these changes drew their strength from the Constitution whose Preamble expresses the solemn resolve to secure 'Justice, social, political and economic to every person.' With all these seemingly positive changes women would seem to be an easy wicket but an analysis of empirical survey clearly brings out that despite all hype and hyperbole life of an Indian women is still regulated, less by Constitutional guarantees and legal measures, and more by traditions, customs and unwritten laws of the days of yore. Manu, the supreme law giver, still seems to control the thinking of the masses.

Gender bias is sanctioned by social values and norms. Gender relations are social relations. They reflect how women are disadvantaged in their access to power, personal autonomy and even safety from physical violence. A man can sow his wild oats the world over and keep a thousand mistresses (provided he can afford them) and be praised for his virility and masculinity but a woman who sleeps once with a man other than the husband is regarded as worse than a whore!

It revealed the convenient penchant of the Government to sweep under the rug some of the most grotesque crimes that are committed against women and to connive with other enforcement agencies in protecting the guilty. Many cases that came to light showed that several women who complained of police atrocities or crimes committed on them were taken to task and treated brutally. The number of such cases is still mounting. This survey has convincingly demonstrated that the bulk of the offenders are never caught due to ineffective implementation of the laws and much less are convicted or imprisoned. Victim surveys and self-reports have provided support to the assertion that the prospective offenders grow bolder by the bleak chances of apprehension and conviction. On a comprehensive analysis of the problems, as specialities of each case came to light directly, generalisations became increasingly difficult to make. It is impossible to de-link the problem of crimes against women from deeper social realities and to analyse the problem of the efficacy of protective laws in seclusion.

Phenomenon like dowry demands, ill treatment of women, sati, eve teasing, superior status of men privileged position of sons and bias against daughters have massive social sanctions behind them and cannot be removed despite progressive laws.

Unfulfilled Constitutional Guarantees

Women have been suppressed for ages through social sanctions, religious cults, physical ad psychic arts. Equality before law and equality of status is more in books than in the mores of the Indian community. Even in the foetus if the sex is identified or at birth when the sex is discovered the females have been put to sleep.

The status of women, their opportunity of employment, their illiteracy and subjugation to men are a negation of the promise of equality. The dignity of women leaves much to be desired, she is still a bonded labour, a gang rape victim, a damsel for sale in the weekly markets in backward states or a commodity to be sold to foreigners as a bride or as a keep for a price. Human dignity crushed by social system is the lot of the Indian woman. Some social consciousness about the status of women and the protective laws has been aroused in recent years by education, mass media and the efforts of the social workers.

The number of protective laws which seek to protect these rights has increased, but when women go to seek redress under these laws it is only the frustrating failures and disappointments that they get in return. An apt example of this reality is the ghastly tragedy in which three sisters committed suicide because their father could not afford the dowry. Earlier the elder sister was paraded before the prospective grooms a number of times and rejected. In a country where there is a full-fledged Act prohibiting dowry and where there are stringent punishments for demanding dowry how could such a thing happen? Obviously the laws remain a force on the paper and are ineffective in practice. These days a greater number of women are killed because of inadequate dowry. Fraud-marriages are performed to squeeze out money from desperate parents, homes break because of greed for more dowry. All this becomes more disturbing because there is an anti-dowry laws which has been amended twice. The rules framed under this Act prescribe setting up of a machinery to monitor the functioning of the Act, but no effort has been made to set up such a machinery. According to Government Rules, giving or taking of dowry, or abetting in the same is prohibited yet it is the high placed Government officials, the Ministers and MPs who lead in flouting these rules. Marriages in their families are performed with a lavish display of wealth and a lot of dowry changes hands.

It is remarkable that according to the ruling of the Supreme Court a woman's Streedhan is a trust with the in-laws and if the marriage breaks she is entitled to get it back within three months, yet when it comes to reclaiming dowry, all sorts of hurdles are created. The girl is driven from pillar to post for years with virtually no assistance from the enforcement machinery. The police cannot take any action unless the in-laws actually refuse to give back the dowry and initiating legal proceedings results in a lot of delay, harassment and mental torture. The financial viability of an indefinite legal proceeding is questionable, moreover streedhan is rarely used for the benefit of the bride.

Socially, it is considered the privilege of the in-laws to utilise it the way they want with the bride having no say whatsoever. Legal action is rarely contemplated against the husband or the in-laws in cases of cruelty. It is still considered shameful to expose family problems. The victim is consoled by telling her that it is a normal happening of every household and making it public will bring nothing but shame and sarcasm.

In very exceptional circumstances does the victim register a complaint. The whole burden falls on the woman to prove her case, which, of course, is too heavy. There are no witnesses to vouch for her. The culprit ensures that they are bribed, blackmailed or else so much harassed by constant adjournments of the case on flimsy grounds and other delaying tactics that they finally give up and are not prepared to testify. Delay in trials also results in disappearance of evidence and loss of sympathy for the woman. All these legal hassles prove the ineffectiveness of the protective laws.

Towards Positive Direction

The legislature seems to have recognised the need for intervention in the private domain of families and introduced significant changes in the law relating to offences against wife; notable among them is Section 498-A IPC, which is streered towards acts of cruelty and Section 376-A IPC dealing with sexual intercourse with a wife who is divorced or separated.

Remarkably, the traditional Hindu Law there was no bar for a man to have more than one wife. A girl was normally married before attaining puberty without taking her consent but under Hindu Marriage Act, 1955 bigamy is made illegal. Earlier whenever there was a marital discord and marriage did not work women were just deserted by their husbands, they could not do anything about it.

Now, Hindu Law permits the wife to make a petition for the restitution of conjugal rights, judicial separation or divorce. Under Hindu Succession Act women can claim property rights. Section 498-A is there to protect the women from harassment for dowry, Section 176 Cr. PC and Section 113-A and 113-B help in the investigation of dowry deaths and dowry related crimes.

Notably, legal enactments in the last few decades have tried to establish a balance between the right to privacy (under which most of the crimes against women were hidden) and social and legal obligations. It has been asserted by the Supreme Court that even in matrimonial cases there is no territory outside the domain of Articles 14, 19 and 21 of the Constitution.

Resistance to Legal Changes

Most of the crimes that are committed against women have become so institutionalised that they are condoned not only by the society and other institutions that are supposed to curb them but also by the victims themselves. In real life people are totally submissive when their daughters are married. They express their helplessness to fight against such a well established custom and follow the traditions. People may keep up a bold front in public but accept dowry on the sly, most of them demand it when their sons get married on pleas like 'it will displease the elders.... it is still a status symbol or .... after all marriage is once in lifetime etc.'

Most of the men possess double personality. 'Either a goddess or a door mat' appeared to be the correct assessment of the actual behaviour of such men with women. They praised women in front of others, gave them the greatest respect and even extended a helping hand to the wife in menial jobs when others were around. They showed their true colours while inter-acting with women in their private life. The growing incidents of eve teasing and sexual harrassment of girls at work place is an appropriate pointer in this direction. Though the exact number of professionals, doctors, lawyers, police officers and service personnel who beat their wives could not be assessed yet the magnitude of this crime that came to light is unbelievable.

Parents and Relatives Responsible for

The parents are biased in their training towards their daughters. They do not teach them independence and self-reliance. Only 30% of the parents asserted that girls should not be submissive and should have some marketable skill before getting married.

There are several boys who succumb to family pressure and marry the girls that their parent's select for getting dowry but later on harass and torture or even kill that girl to get married to their girl friend. There are cases where the parents and relatives sell their proteges to pimps or brothel owners for prostitution. There are husbands who are dupe their wives in flesh trade or force them to act in blue films. In a case filed by Suraj in Crimes (Women) Cell the victim was a professional married to a Doctor. Barely four days after the marriage, his brother-in-law started taking undue liberties with the girl. She complained to her husband. But instead of supporting her, the husband beat her for being too conservative.

Later on, learning that the brother-in-law had tried to rape Suraj, the husband expressed shock, not on the conduct of his brother-in-law but on the conservative nature of the girl in not being able to take small flings of life in a lighter vein. Her own husband tried to buy time by telling her that he will sort out the matter.

When she expressed her determination to report the case, she was threatened with desertion. This threat proved to be too overbearing but ultimately when neither the beatings not the advances by the brother-in-law stopped she was forced to report. It was revealed on investigation that the doctor had married her without any serious intentions, his main aim was to sell off the wife to his brother-in-law who had obliged him with a loan for buying a house. The Crime Cell refused to lodge a complaint of rape as a lot of time had elapsed and no medical was done.

Gradual Change in Perception

Observations revealed that men cannot be objective because they have grown up in certain grooves of thought as privileged members of the family. But a perceptible change was noted in the thinking of some men (17.3% of those who were interviewed). These were the men who were educated and interacted with the oppressed women directly. "I was educated and interacted with the oppressed women directly. "I was a typical male chauvinist," they agreed, "but the growing number of cases of excesses that come to us, the brutality with the crimes are committed, have brought about this change."

A reasonable level of support for victimised women has started coming from a section of the media, legal profession, and at times by interpretation of laws and giving judgments favourable to women. There has been a realisation that the women cannot live like human beings unless suitable legal enactments are vigorously enforced to protect them.

A survey has conclusively proved that the change in perception has not been accompanied by faith, the faith that the society will not castigate the victims and the law enforcement authorities will cooperate with them. Women still do not want to approach the police for help because of the fear of harassment. The social sigma attached to crimes like rape, prostitution, bigamy, molestation, etc. compounds their problems.

During the trials, various very personal and embarrassing questions are asked, it deters women from reporting offences, making the existence of protective laws irrelevant. The Crimes (Women) Cells were set up in some States as an experiment, to create greater confidence and to simplify the legal procedure yet the problem has not shown any appreciable change in the outlook of the women who approach the Cell mostly in extreme circumstances.

Probably women do not have the confidence to complain. They know by experience that reporting will only complicate their problems. The experiences of women who have complained are not very happy, although the five year plans and other development projects have provided improved services and facilities in terms of education, training employment, health, family welfare etc. and have helped women in improving their status yet the majority of women are still receiving humiliating, oppressive and sometimes cruel treatment, which is more common in the backward and lower castes and also in the neo rich middle class, who have still not been able to break loose mentally from the age old taboos and value system.

In all the cases of crimes, women are in a highly disadvantageous position. Such crimes are mostly unilateral and without any provocation but there are some cases, about 13% where the wives are totally unreasonable or they share the fault. In most of the other cases they are extra considerate. In a large number of cases of bride burning, the dying women had made a declaration giving a clean chit to her husband. She invariably said that she caught fire in an accident. There are many reported cases which prove this. A survey of the decided cases shows that in a majority of the cases, if a dying declaration absolving the husband is made, the police do not investigate the case further for any foul play or additional clues and the judges acquit the convict on the strength of the declaration.

Fear psychosis is another reason for not reporting. The culprits blackmail the woman or create a conviction that the law is impotent, police are corrupt and the process of law very expensive, long and unending, so she will not gain anything by reporting against him. The victims are scared of the relatives and friends who will come to know about the case and look down upon them. The wife is convinced that the husband will make her life miserable if he comes to know that she has told anyone about his misbehaviour, and convinces the woman that he is not bothered about the legal consequences. Often, the culprit on getting an inkling that the wife may report against him, starts creating evidence in his favour by bribing the police and requesting his colleagues to give evidence in his favour. He virtually starts a vicious campaign telling people that the wife is selfish and lazy.

She does not care for him or she is too haughty and arrogant and does not respect his parents etc. In two cases the offender had beaten himself with the same object with which he had brutally beaten his wife and told the police that he had only reacted in self-defence.

In one of the representative cases, the husband, a class one Government officer, beat his IAS wife brutally in front of her peon. He openly told her that he will frame the evidence against her for having soft feelings for the peon if she ever reported the matter.

He refused to take her to a Government doctor till she gave in writing that she had got hurt accidentally by falling from the stairs. It was very difficult to consider any action against the husband by the wife at that stage.

Women's organisations help only initially, their help is just a publicity stunt, they leave the woman midway. Protective homes are not proper places for respectable ladies. Mostly prostitutes and women of doubtful character live there. Women, who have gone there as the last desperate resort are very soon disillusioned; they want to get out of them. Nothing much has changed in spite of repeated strictures by the Supreme Court about their pathetic condition.

Working and self-sufficient women are more exposed

to the adverse publicity. They face more problems of adjustment. They have less time to indulge in family politics and create favourable opinion for themselves.

The case of raped women is worse because rape is not just physical violence or injury, its significance lies in the physical repugnance, the mental and emotional trauma and the severe social repercussions. Each time a rape takes place, the woman becomes a socially ostracized victim of assault. In the process she creases to be a person or a social being she merely becomes a rape victim.

In most of the cases, even the parents and the relations of the girls, advised them to be more tolerant and forgiving and to avoid confrontation. In about half the cases where the girl was beaten up and turned out of the house most insultingly, the parents wanted the girls to patch up with the erring husband when feelers were sent by the husband through some common friend or relations. In cases where the husband himself came to patch up, the parents were to happy and almost compelled the girl to swallow her pride and agree for a settlement. There were several cases where the girls repeatedly shunted from their husbands house to the parents house and had finally died a tragic death.

Remarkably, most surprising were the cases of those girls who were educated and independent, and were earning well, yet they submitted to the beatings and tortures of the husband. The statistics may show the figure of such women as negligible but the survey by the researcher showed that the number of working women who were cried against was much more than non-working women. There were few cases where the educated working wife was battered most mercilessly for days together, insulted, taunted, starved and finally forced to get out, still she wanted to be accepted back by the husband that too on his own terms, though the husband, even then, was not at all inclined to do that. The case of Malini is typical of this class, it is quite an eye-opener. She was an educated graduate girl from the family of a very rich businessman. Her father gave almost everything in dowry including tickets for a Continental tour for the honeymoon and a brand new Maruti. Malini was very happy for the initial few days but soon the taunts started. According to Malini, the main culprit for starting the dissensions in their happy life was the mother-in-law. She instigated her son to tame his high headed wife. The beatings and torture were so brutal that twice the parents lodged complaints with the police but later on withdrew them, on an assurance by the husband.

The husband did not change, he filed a suit for divorce. Malini was still willing to go back on the husbands, terms if he accepted her, but he did not. There are reported cases of judges, doctors, and defence personnel beating their IAS and Doctor wives, and the latter torturing them for years. The amended Dowry Act makes the concept of dowry wider and provides for extra police intervention in handling dowry cases. In 1986 with the insertion of Section 304-B in the Penal Code dowry death has become a specific crime and the presumptions incorporated in the Evidence Act made it easier to implicate the culprits.

They need not actually commit the murder or abet it in the 'traditional sense,' yet the amendments have failed to prevent harassment and torture for dowry nor have they reduced the growing number of dowry deaths.

In several cases litigation had commenced in a fit of anger and was being contested in a spirit of revenge. All the issues involved could have been settled by friendly talks yet were being litigated upon for years because once the case goes to the courts, the attitudes harden and the party that had committed the wrong maintains unfair advantage till the case is settled.

Legal Provisions' Inadequacy

A critical examination of the legal provisions revealed that most of the protective laws for women suffer from various loopholes or shortcomings. They are complicated and ambiguous, and instead of solving the issues make the situation more complex. Often the provisions of the law are not clear and precise, it makes them the soleground for legal interpretation in the hierarchy of courts.

Certain laws remain confined to statue books, because the enforcement machinery is inadequate, or the penalties are not awarded according in the stipulations.

Many of these protective laws like the Act prohibiting Sati were passed in such a great hurry that there was no time even to think about the various aspects of the enactment. Indecent representation of Women is a classic example of a hurriedly passed law. The act was passed with a lot of urgency yet the rules implementing that law were not made for years. This shows the callows attitude of the executive and the unenthusiastic reaction of the aforcement authorities.

The Dowry (Prohibition) Act is just one example of the consumable acts which do not take into account the social realities of a woman's life. Such laws can only be a palliative measure to near the State out of a problem and help it to get out of an ugly motion by appeasing a particular group of people.

The laws on Sati and Cruelty against Married Women

are some other examples of laws which cannot be enforced effectively. The law on Sati is heartless it treat Sati as a case of suicide. The definition of jurification of Sati is vague and ambiguous, which gives place to kindness. In spite of a number of changes in the laws, the dowry problem not only continues, but has assumed alarming proportions. It has even spread to communities where it did not exist, thereby putting the efficacy of the system in doubt. The continued differences in various personal laws and absence of adequate enforcement mechanisms has made many of the other laws ineffective.

Many upcoming crimes, despite the havoc caused by their increasing incidents, are not even perceived as a crime, e.g. dowry deaths were treated as accidental deaths for years, wife beating is still not recognised as a specific crime. It is provided for under the general law on assault. Cruelty to wife by the husband or the in-laws has been declared a crime under Section 498-A IPC, but the definition of cruelty is quite vague. It has left several vital aspects of cruelty out of the purview of the law. Discussions with the victims bring out that in most of the cases, the reasons for the cruel treatment of the wife was not dowry, it is suspicion of illicit sexual relations, mutual incompatibility or a girl friend yet the enforcement authorities show reluctance to register crimes on these grounds.

Remarkably, it was only in March 1991 the personnel of Crimes (Women) Cell were instructed to give a liberal interpretator to Section 498-A and register cases of wife beating and harassment irrespective of dowry demands. The procedural requirement of Section 498-A, that only the woman victim, her parents or relations by blood can file a complaint make it very difficult for the victim to get a complaint lodged in critical cases.

As such amended Act on Prostitution remains a paper tiger because there is no responsible agency to monitor its use or abuse. The Act neglects the root cause of this evil. It has failed to plug the supply and the demand position in the flesh market which remains unchanged. In fact, the new Act has only pushed the trade underground, but it is flourishing nevertheless.

The Call girl culture, liaison girls, use of female figures in the advertisement of consumer products, all ensure renewed life to this profession because the Act neither prohibits prostitution altogether nor gives legitimacy to promiscuous sex activity; by keeping a neutral attitude to the profession itself, the act seeks to identify and deal with the crimes connected with it. The law starts with the presumption that it is an inevitable evil and cannot be curbed. It treats prostitutes, the victim of social injustice, as criminals and is silent on the punishment of those who hire them.

It is pertinent to girls are either raped or molested and then sold into the business. Sometimes extreme poverty forces them to take to prostitution. There were instances of channelising young girls into prostitution through religious and cultural sanctions also.

Some of the laws which were passed after much deliberation and thinking are no better. The anti-women bias is easily perceptible. Probably the pro-male lobby does not accept the liberal changes. The rape laws are an apt example of such laws. After the furore of *Mathura Rape case,* a Law Commission was set up to study the demands of various sections of the society regarding changes in the outdated rape laws which had existed on the Code since 1860 and were against the Indian culture and ethos.

The recommendations of the Law Commission included the demand 'that the woman's past history and general conduct should not be used as evidence and the onus of proof that the woman did not consent should be on the accused.' The Commission also recommended some pretrial procedures and made police officer's refusal to register a complaint, an offence. However, the Bill which was presented to the Parliament in August 1980, did not include any of these positive recommendations. The present rape laws do not even take into account cases of marital rape. The undue emphasis on the character of the prosecutrix is a real boon to the rapist. A rape is a rape. Why should the character of the woman raped be considered?

After the amendments it was expected what the courts would follow the spirit of the amendment and give women a better deal. But that hope has been belied. There are a large number of cases where the culprit has been treated very leniently, e.g. in *Suman Rani's case* the Supreme Court reduced the sentence from 10 years in 5 years and rejected the review petition filed by the women's groups against the reduction of the sentence.

The amendments made in the Criminal Procedure Code, Indian Penal Code and the Indian Evidence Act are merely an eyewash. Several judgments pronounced before these amendments are more progressive than the ones in later years after the changes. The most relevant is the fact that the law even before the amendments could have been interpreted progressively if the courts so wished, e.g. in *Harpal Singh* v. *State of Himachal Pradesh* a sixteen year old girl was gang raped. The apex court ruled that the girl is used to sexual recourse is immaterial in a rape trial. Contrast this judgment with the verdict given in *Suman Rani's Case.* In Indian conditions, it is very rare for a woman or a girl to make false allegations of rape yet a woman's credibility and veracity is always open to suspicion. This is clearly reflected in the existing rape laws and the judgments pronounced by various courts.

The inability of the legislature to pass an effective law banning various sex determination tests and resultant death of girls even before birth have added to the woes of women. There is no specific law to protect women against sexual harassment at the work place. An overview of the decided case shows that judges, who can make these laws more effective by a positive approach are equally insensitive. They allow cases of crimes against women to be adjourned on frivolous grounds. It is normal for cases of marital cruelty, eve teasing and sexual harassment to drag on for years.

There seems to be total lack of empathetic laws favouring battered women of a broken marriage or a sufferer of an unhealthy and diseased marriage. Battered women struggle in the courts for years before they can get justice.

The increasing demands of evidence by the courts ensures that many persons come out innocent. The courts do not realise the compulsion of a woman and her difficulty in proving the crimes. Our criminal jurisprudence is oriented towards ocular testimony so a lot hinges on what the witnesses say, but producing a witness in the court to testify for the woman is like dragging a bull by its horns.

The rules of evidence are faulty. A lot of preferential treatment is given to the culprit but no one seems to be bothered about the victim, the person for whose benefit the whole system of criminal jurisprudence exists. Law does not take notice of the fact that there are especial types of crimes of which only women are the victims and which cannot be proved by our traditional legal system. Every crime against women cannot be proved beyond reasonable doubt. There cannot be legally accepted proof for every such crime.

A woman victim has to go from pillar to post to know the sources of legal aid, and to find out an efficient lawyer. The survey showed that the knowledge about legal enactments is very scant, not only amongst the poor and the illiterate women but amongst the educated women like executives, teachers, office workers and also amongst the men. Majority of the subjects, both men and women, who were questioned opined that the whole subject of law is so complicated and vast that it is not possible to understand it, 61% of the law students found the laws to be too confusing. 86% women were of the opinion that 'there is no point studying the legal enactments and getting confused God forbid, if something happens we will go to the lawyers.... In any case we have to engage the lawyers even if we have some knowledge of law.'

There were some enactments like Sati, Child Marriage Restraint Act and Dowry Act about which there was general awareness 95% of the people knew about them, but they were neither aware of the exact nomenclature nor the details of the provisions. The source of their knowledge was TV serials, radio, newspapers and magazines. The knowledge about the procedural aspect was almost nil 98.6% of the subjects did not know about it. The educated litigants knew about the particular Sections, punishment, and relief which they could get.

These women frankly admitted that they had become wise after the tragedy, had they known about the law earlier they would have collected ample proofs and would not have been deceived by the culprits. The lack of awareness of sources of legal aid was almost 83%. There was the vague reply that the police and the courts are the institutions for getting justice but there was ignorance about the procedure to be followed. A lot of confusion and ignorance about laws was observed even amongst those who were charged with implementing these laws. Immoral Traffic (Prevention) Act was passed in 1986 but cases continued to be booked under SITA for at least four years after that because the policemen who register the cases at the police station did not know about the new enactment.

The experiences of women with the enforcement machinery are not very happy. Most of them, disappointed with the obstructive role of the police, the problems faced in hiring an efficient and knowledgeable lawyers and the tardy pace at which the case proceeded. Only 6% of the women, who belonged to the upper strata of the society were satisfied. They could perhaps exert some influence and get speedier justice. Some women narrated in detail the difficulties in getting a good advocate and also told how the lawyers left no opportunity of fleecing them. These women expressed horror at the large number if adjournments of their cases and the courts bowing to the delaying tactics of the culprits.

Generally, 93% of the women victims felt let down by a system which promises so much yet gives so little. 'That is why crimes are increasing,' some of them said in desperation, 'more and more people are resorting to self-help. Such people are perhaps happier even if they fail.... at least their conscience is at ease... they have done their mite. We, being women cannot do it. The judges just don't realise our plight and give adjournments even without giving us an opportunity to tell them about our plight or to prove that the culprit is not appearing just to harass us or to take advantage of our helplessness.

'It is not worth all the harassment and the expenditure that we had to undergo. Laws should be simple and the remedies quick,' they said without being asked. Ameena who made the headlines was not happy. She confided that the extra attention that she got has made her the odd man out in her community, it should be like this for everyone. She also felt that the legal process was too long and complicated.

Monisha Verma who was molested by the three DTC employees in 1988 and was successful in getting all the three culprits punished felt that women should not be afraid. "Ten years imprisonment will act as a solid deterrent to a any kind of harassment. It should make men wary and women confident to know that the law favours the truth." Women should not cringe' was the opinion of Mukti Datta who had filed a case against the Minister of Environment. Mukti had to do it alone, as all the initial liberal help by women's organisation faded into the thin air after the initial enthusiasm, but she was not deterred by the adversities. It is beside the point that ultimately she compromised with the culprit as a mark of respect for the old and sick man.

It is pertinent to note that women who had initiated the legal process but had left it half way through, confided that it is very difficult to prove the charges in a court. The culprit blackmails the witnesses and they turn hostile, so no crime can ever be proved, moreover, the time consuming legal process, harassment and expenditure involved is not worth. The lawyers charge lot of money on each date but the case simply does not move. Such women repented why wisdom had not dawned on them earlier when experienced people told them not to rely on promises held out by codified law. 'Nothing can be gained even at the end of the legal marathon.'

Protective laws may declare bigamy to be a crime and rape a serious offence for which the minimum sentence is seven years but the law in action may punish the culprit till the rising of the court even after the offence of rape is proved beyond reasonable doubts!

The court does not agree that the second marriage is performed unless solid proofs of the solemnisation of marriage are given, said some desperate women. What can be greater proof than the fact that our husband is living with another women and ill-treats us when we raise our voice against the relationship? Such women appeared to be totally demoralised and defeated.

Most of the women were disappointed with the rude behaviour of the police force towards them. Police doubted their statements in every case, be it torture, sexual harrassment, eve teasing or rape. 'What is proof,' seemed to be the refrain of the police in all complaints. Certain complaints like wife beating and eve teasing, were taken by the police rather casually, they wanted to dismiss them as too trivial. Police take full advantage of the loopholes and short comings of the law enforcement machinery to discourage them from lodging complaints.

The police cite examples to convince them that in spite of all efforts at their level the culprit does not get convicted. 'There is lot of resistance in getting serious offences registered' told a large number of victims, some of them, about 37% even asserted that their cases were not registered because the culprits had already approached the police and had agreed to give money to them if they helped them to get out of the situation, 21% complained that the police registering the complaint recorded the complaint after they agreed to omit the names of some of the culprits or make changes in the complaint.

There were complaints against the police making additions while writing the FIR to make serious offences look trivial. In most of the cases of cruelty and harassment the police convince the victim that it is not point washing dirty linen in public because cruelty and torture can never be proved. It is better to withdraw the case and patch up. They take it for granted that it is the woman's fault and ask 'what did not do to make the husband annoyed,' they tell her to be loving and forgiving eve it is not her fault. Cases of eve teasing are taken in a very light vain and the culprits are let off with only a warning or some beating.

As such the experiences of women with the police at the thana level have not been very happy. 'At senior level they are usually helpful' was the view of some women, 'but then how many of us can approach them and how many times?' 82% women faced lot of difficulties at the police stations. Widows, poor women and members of the scheduled castes were harassed by being called to the police station repeatedly, and all regulations of not arresting women in the night and questioning them in the presence of a woman constable were flouted. They were troubled when they went to register complaints against their husbands or some other influential persons.

Such women, if they were from the poor strata, were arrested on trumped up charges and tortured. The interview of women, who had lodged complaints against atrocities by husband, or eve teasing and rape etc., revealed the dissatisfaction with the way the police works. 'These policemen are not bothered by the chances of their being reported to the seniors, or of their activities being made public.' In the month of May 1992, in South Delhi's Lajpat Nagar, a sub-inspector was dismissed, after he tried to coerce a woman, who had gone to lodge a complaint against her husband, into flesh trade. The victim in this case was somewhat lucky—the matter was raised in Parliament by a sympathetic member so the police top-brass swung into action, immediately dismissing the sub-inspector an ordering a departmental probe against him.

The Additional Commissioner was furious that such a thing should happen in an area under his jurisdiction. On being interviewed he admitted that there appeared to be some degree of connivance in the sordid business. He said that efforts would be made to ascertain whether such a thing had happened in the thana earlier also. Fortunately the experiences of women with the Women Cell are happy as far as listening to their complaints sympathetically and registering cases are concerned. It is after the husband is called to the Cell that string pulling sometimes starts.

There are many examples of the cases being spoilt at the FIR stage by the police. Police treat dowry death cases as a lottery. It gives them an opportunity to make contacts with influential persons. They avoid arresting the culprit. It helps him in blackmailing the witnesses. The offender can contact influential persons or remain absconding till the initial enthusiasm and sympathy for the victim evaporates. It is the same in rape cases also.

The corruption and indifference at the investigation level and all the stage of preparing the charge sheet is phenomenal. The time taken for investigation is too long and often evidence is destroyed by the time the investigation starts. Most of the policemen who investigate the cases have neither specialised skills in investigations nor do they have legal knowledge. They are not aware of the questions that will be put to them by the courts.

A survey has shown that the police treat crimes against women as low profile and risky jobs. About 66% of the women who had sought police help, specially in crimes like cruelty, eve teasing, etc. asked the police to drop the charges after the investigation had started or positive proofs of the guilt of the accused had started coming to light. The reasons for withdrawing the charges were genuine. Mostly husbands try to buy peace by assurances of good behaviour and threaten further violence if their requests are not conceded to, otherwise also the women do not want their husbands to be imprisoned or treated harshly.

Non-availability of proper legal advice or guidance was a great handicap for women in distress. The lawyers, instead of reaching out to such women, exploit and prey upon them. The majority of the advocates are most casual about the case, they are only interested in making out a *prima facie* case sufficient to have the matter admitted or an interim order granted. Their sole aim seems to be a desire to make money. Most of them are unprincipled, unethical and unprofessional. Professional dishonesty was found to be on the increase. Most of the lawyers charge extra fees by telling the women that it is not the law or facts on the basis of which a case is decided. It is the discretion of the judge that is going to save the victim. It has its price so money is needed to purchase it. Money, influence, old associations almost everything is used to obtain favour for the client.

The non-availability of proper legal aid and guidance proves to be a real road-block. Some advocates openly tell their clients to break the witnesses. There is a lot of lawyer stimulated litigation. Cases which could have been solved amicably linger on for years. Lawyers are in a big way responsible for denial of speedy justice. They refuse to subordinate their selfish interests to that of their clients resulting in years of delays and denials of justice.

Nearly 83% of the women complained of the impersonal attitude of the judges. 'The judges, whether a man or a woman, do not seem to be sympathetic to our plight,' told most of the victims of rape, cruelty, prostitution, etc. 'They seem to be oblivious of the trauma that we, the victims of heinous crimes like rape or sexual violence undergo, and the time it takes to recoup from the horrifying experience.... The delay in lodging the FIR is seen by the courts as a material to doubt our testimony.' The judges do not realise that it does take time for a woman to muster enough strength and support for the registration of a case which is socially stigmatized.

The case with which serious cases of crimes against women are adjourned and long dates are given frustrate the victims. The release of persons, charged with heinous crimes, on bail and anticipatory bail has a very demoralising effect on the victim. The freedom after getting a bail is normally used to circumvent the due process of justice.

Misuse of Law

It was noticed during the survey, that there are some misguided elements amongst women who misuse the law to reap vengeance and harass the poor husband. According to a lady magistrate Prabha Tak, who has lot of experience of cases of dowry deaths, "young girls marry with lot of aspirations based on movies and films. Their expectations are totally unrealistic, they are away from the mundane realities of life, this leads to tensions and frustrations when realities dawn after marriage. The new culture of not teaching the girls any if the household jobs makes their lives miserable. They have not learnt cooking naturally their clothes will catch fire if they are not careful." Similar are views of DCP Crime (Women) Cell and many of the men who were interviewed. Most of the cases of dowry harassment are actually cases of marital maladjustment. The wife commits suicide out of frustration of work or because of her inability to make adjustments. and the poor husband and his family have to take the blame and suffer the stigma. Sometimes he has to take the blame for the acts of his over-sentimental wife. The girl's parents, by blaming the in-laws for demanding more dowry or perpetrating atrocities, actually cover up their own responsibility of not bringing up their daughters properly. At times parents marry their daughter against her wishes and the poor husband has to suffer the consequences of marrying an unwilling wife or a girl who is not compatible.

Increasing Incidence of Crimes Against Women

The graph of crimes against women is galloping at a very fast pace, but the authorities instead of doing anything concrete keep passing the responsibility from one authority to another, e.g. in 1992, the Minister of State of Home after rattling out the figures in Parliament, washed off his hands by telling the members that registration, investigation, and prevention of crime was a state subject. "We have amended the Dowry Prohibition Act and other Acts related to women, rest is up to the States." This statement itself shows the casual attitude of the executive. These amendments were made way back in 1986 and some were made even earlier, and in 1992 the Minister was harping upon them as if they were recent changes. This information was not criticised by any of hon'ble member of the Parliament.

Sharp Rise in Crimes by Juveniles

Delinquency by juveniles and those just past the age of 18 was generally considered an exception, but all crimes particularly crimes like rape, sexual harassment and eve teasing, committed by boys up to the age of 18-20 shot up significantly in the two years.

Out of 61.27 lakh crimes registered officially throughout the country in 1990 over 32.87 lakh were committed by boys under 30 years of age. In metros like Delhi and Bombay as many as 70% of those arrested for various crimes are under 25 years. According to one Deputy Commissioner of Police "Today's major criminals are aged between 18 to 22." Ruthless youngsters are seeing crime as a way of life. The reason for this rise is the sense of insecurity in the child, parental neglect and more exposure to life without proper guidance from school and parents. The misplaced sympathy and lenient attitude of the enforcement authorities towards the juvenile has also encouraged the prospective offenders.

The courts also seem oblivious of this emerging phenomenon and award very lenient punishment to the offenders, their logic being that a long-term in jail and the company of other criminals will turn the juveniles into obdurate criminals. This logic may sound correct but the remedy lies in prison reforms and segregation of criminals and not in lenient punishment which encourages other youngster to commit crimes just for a kick.

A survey of statistics of crimes against women shows that every year the number of crimes is spiralling higher and higher. The statistics regarding crimes against women, wheather complied by Crime Record Bureau, Bureau of Police Research and Development, Crimes (Women) Cell, or the figures presented in Parliament from time to time are not very reliable. There is a lot of discrepancy in the data delved out by these agencies; their figures do not tally with each other moreover, they record only the reported incidents of crimes. This hides the reality; the reported crimes form a very small fraction (about 10%) of the actual number of crimes: the statistics neither give us a correct estimate of the volume of the crimes that are committed nor their intensity. The grey area of the crimes are totally neglected, e.g. torture and battering of wives is very common yet the figures convince us that it is a crime not even worth reporting or taking cognizance of.

Women are not inclined to report these crimes due to public apathy and distrust in the enforcement machinery. The social stigma attached to crimes like rape and molestation overcomes the grief and rage of the victim. Uncomfortable cross-questioning by the police, the judiciary and constant pressure from the heartless surrounding force the victim to succumb to the pressures and allow the culprit to get away. They are convinced that approach by influential persons will reduce the chances of a fair trial. At times lack of reporting facilities frustrates women who want to report these crimes in the heat of emotions.

Members of the lower caste have the greatest risk of being disproportionately reported and imprisoned compared to middle and upper class segments of the population. If an accurate analysis of the unreported crimes could be made the apparent differentiation will level out. Crimes against women are more or less evenly distributed throughout the socio-economic structure of society.

According to official figures, all violent crimes against women like rape, all violent crimes against women like rape, cruelty, kidnapping and abduction, prostitution, etc. are increasing. Altogether 57,414 cases of crimes against women were reported from all over the country in 1991 (till November). Madhya Pradesh headed the list with 11,010 followed by UP (9,295) and Rajasthan (4,622). Dowry deaths showed a frightening rise of 800 in just one year. The reported rape cases doubled in the just one decade. This is the reality when over 90% of such cases are not even reported and a mere 1% of end up in conviction. Cases of molestation have gone up from 8,706 in 1988 to 9,517 in 1990, kidnapping and abduction cases were also on the rise from 9,633 in 1988 they went to 11,869 in 1990.

According to the information given by the Minister of State for Home in Rajya Sabha there has been a rise of 11.5% in the overall crime rate in Delhi in the last 6 months of 1991, measures taken by the administration to check the rise of crimes in the Capital included police patrols and posting of additional pickets at sensitive places.

Child abuse and sexual assault on adult women cuts across all strata of society. The boom in media, both print and electronic, has now zoomed the attention of the social scientists, the police, the judiciary and the man on the street on the crimes against women and more victims are coming out and narrating their versions of the trauma.

It was observed that in spite of the phenomenal rise in the number of crimes there is a general decline in the number of convictions; perhaps the reason lies in the large number of arrears. The Judges and Magistrates who sit in the courts crammed with pending cases, are overworked. They have found an easy way out by taking up only simple cases and leaving other cases pending.

The delay in trials makes the victims demoralised and

frustrated. They are no longer interested in pursuing the case. The police is callous in collecting the evidence and recording the statements of the witnesses. The quality of prosecution has also deteriorated. The lawyers are inefficient and unprofessional, they are only interested in collecting money. All these factors result in a very poor rate of conviction in criminal cases.

The statistical survey of the disposal of cases by the enforcement agencies showed the large number of cases that are filed each year and the inability of the authorities to dispose them expeditiously.

A total number of 19,86,266 IPC including the pending cases carried forward from the previous year were taken up for investigation by the police in 1990. Out of these 15,96,960 (80.4%) cases were disposed of by the police and 3,89,306 (19.6%) cases remained pending for investigation at the end of 1990. The break up being 'Charge Sheets' laid in 52.2% cases, 'Final Report True' submitted in 22.2%, 'Charges Found False/Mistake of Law' in 5.5% and 'Investigation Refused' 0.5%.

There were 37,24,566 cases for trial during 1990 including the pending cases, out of which only 8,37,964 (22.5%) were disposed of leaving 28,86,602 (77.5%) cases pending disposal at the end of the year. The disposal of 22.5% was made up of 8.5% cases of conviction, 8.9% cases of acquittal and 5.1% cases compounded or withdrawn.

It was found that most of the cases which are withdrawn on various pretexts like mistake of law or reported as 'found to be false' are generally not so in reality. The women who register these cases are forced by various social pressures, blackmailing tactics of the culprits or the compulsion of circumstances to give in writing that the cases were falsely registered or that they have no grievance against the culprit whatsoever.

A critical analysis shows that the crime situation has worsened over the years. The large number of cases that are registered proves that the hesitation regarding reporting these crimes is perhaps breaking down. Today, more women are mustering up courage to report cases of crimes against themselves and seek redressal. The nationwide campaigns by women's groups on the horrifying rapes of Maya Tyagi, Ramizabi and Gunta Behn, the laws enacted by the Government and the attention focused by the media, have created a climate more favourable to reporting of crimes than it was about a decade ago. Women's organisations are creating legal awareness and taking up the issues with the police and the courts.

The offenders and the society take most of the crimes against women very lightly. There are umpteen number of cases where the husband charged with beating and ill-treating the wife told very casually that the wife got what she deserved. In some other cases the offender is not at all repentant and told in a matter of fact manner that he was forced to marry against his wishes so in spite of his best efforts he could not break away with the former girl friend.... He should not be held to be guilty if the unwanted wife becomes the target if this frustration. Even serious crimes like prostitution and bigamy were justified on grounds of the promiscuous nature of man. Native vice and sexual frustration with the wife. In a recent case in March 1992, the son of a well to do contractor, was so irritated on a triviality that he dragged his wife by the hair and threw her down from the fourth floor, in full view of the neighbours, who had come out hearing the commission. The husband seemed unrepentant even after the event.

In another case a doctor had killed his wife on the same ground in a similar manner. Unfortunately for the doctor, the eight year old son of a neighbour, who had seen the whole incident became an eyewitness. The twists and turns that the case took revealed the weakness of our legal system and the hurdles that come in the way of justice. Initially the police refused to register the case as a murder case. It was registered as a case of accidental death. The boy who had seen the gruesome act was kidnapped and even threatened to be killed. It took seven years for the case to be decided in the Sessions Court and while in jail the Doctor was flooded with offers of marriage by desperate parents.

Eve teasing is generally recognised to be a light hearted sport and sexual harassment of women at work-place is treated as something to be taken in the stride without much fuss. The humiliations and insults heaped on women is always treated as a triviality. Dowry and sati ware justified on grounds of religion and tradition. Wife beating, and bigamy are treated as private affairs and a hush hush crime.

Youths with incomplete lives indulge into deviant behaviour with women to gratify themselves. The danger of crimes makes them feel alive. The fear of law has gone. Some trials take place after years. With the collapse of the judicial system people believe that the crime pays.

Enforcement Agencies

It was observed that the enforcement agencies, the police advocates, and the courts share a great portion of the blame for the inefficient implementation of the protective laws.

Police Role

Quite a few Policemen were guilty of not doing their duties properly. Normally a junior rank police officer decides whether a case will be registered, or not, if he refuses to register it, in 99% cases that case dies a natural death.

The gradual conversion of the police force into a VIP security force resulted in mass exodus of efficient police officers and inept handling of crime cases by inexperienced officials. This has generated bad publicity, adverse judicial observations and frustrations. The shortage of personnel has also contributed to this sorry state of affairs. Anything connected with politics becomes a mega affair and policemen are drafted from all the stations. This has reduced the availability of the police force for protective, preventive and detective work at the station level. This invariably results in neglect of routine work The shortage of head constables, SIs and inspectors has made the situation worse.

Most of the women are scared to go to the police station to report crimes being committed against them. They have no faith in the police. According to a Judge of Allahabad High Court, "the police is the most organised group of criminals in uniform," some other police officers have expressed similar opinions.

The policemen are involved in cases ranging from eve teasing, wife beating to heinous crimes like rape and murder. The Peoples Union For Democratic Rights (PUDR) and Amnesty International have also cast aspersions on the criminal behaviour of the police: their involvement in custodial rape, and their corrupt way of working.

Senior police officials with whom discussions were held appeared to be at a loss over the increasing evidence which suggest criminalisation of police ranks. They asserted that the guilty cops are being dealt with promptly and firmly but agreed that this has somehow failed to stem the rot.

In recent years the standard of the police force has been falling and discipline seems to be a thing of the past. The IPS officers have lost their dignity. They believe more in publicity than in doing any real job. Every senior police officer seems to be in search of some god father from amongst the political bosses.

Most of the police personnel found guilty by the organisation were below the rank of Assistant Sub-Inspectors (ASIs). It is not because officers of the higher rank are less guilty but because there is a foolproof system of protecting them. They enjoy political patronage. Some junior level officers are made the sacrificial lamb for the faults of the seniors. In certain cases where departmental inquiries were initiated against the guilty police officers there was no follow up action and despite inquiries they continued to be in service. In a particular case a head constable was caught in eve teasing thrice but no punitive action was taken against him.

The police uniform has given the cops a false sense of security and the system insulates them from any kind of harm. No one is prepared to testify against them. The judicial-system is slow, it gives him ample time to wipe out all evidence against him. Case records reflect police's protective attitude towards their colleagues. There is always an initial reluctance to register cases against the police personnel and cases against them are withdrawn from the court without even framing the charge sheet. Policemen are usually not arrested, they are released on bail before the trial often on technical grounds.

Conviction of cops committing crimes is very rare.

Instead of taking effective measures to prevent women from becoming a prey to police outrage and taking measures to redress them, the authorities try to cover up such cases. Local officers have often refused to receive complaints of police abuses and they even deny that such abuses have even occurred. They do not try to find out the reality even at the departmental level, to pull up the recalcitrant cop. In rare cases where the police have been found guilty, punishment has been lax.

Most of the crimes against women are committed by known culprits yet the policeman usually fail to collect evidence which will prove their guilt. This is the reality despite the assertion of the Police Commissioner of Delhi that notwithstanding the pressures and tensions, the Delhi Police has made significant improvements in their technique of investigation. The police either mess up the case or fail to produce what it takes to get a criminal convicted.

Police people blame the rules of evidence which rely so heavily on the evidence of the witnesses. Sections 25 and 26 of the Evidence Act also handicaps the police. The statement of a witness to the police is an unsigned note and becomes useless the moment a witness turns hostile. In spite of modernising the Delhi Police their investigations are not at all scientific. Most of the Assistant Commissioners of Police (ACPs) and SHOs have no grasp of legal matters so they fail to foresee what can transpire in the court. It was observed that often, when the case is presented at the Sessions Court, the prosecutor is rarely present and a policeman argues the charge.

The investigating officer is not present either. Any information sought by the judge is presented by the defence counsel or a policeman. The family members of the victim are rarely informed about the date of hearing by the police. The police have distanced themselves from the public by their corrupt ways of working and rude behaviour. There are several instances where clear cases of murder are closed by the police as cases of accidental death, e.g. in Tripta Sharma's case. There were 50% burns on her hands, abdomen, thighs and cheeks.

The police held that they were caused by the falling of the kerosene lamp at her in-laws place and ignoring obvious circumstantial evidence, they closed the case. It was due to the perseverance of her parents that the Supreme Court ultimately issued notice to the SSP to reopen the case and make thorough investigations in this *prima facie* case.

The Lawyers

The lawyers are a vital link in the chain of justice but they have not done their bit in making the enforcement of protective laws effective. They are too demanding from their clients for the real or imaginary work that they undertake. Their effort is to prolong the issue on various pretexts so that they can ask for more money. They actually charge money for each date irrespective of the fact that there was no hearing.

The frequent strikes by lawyers have caused havoc. Each day lawyers strike work for a day at least 10,000 cases are added to what has become an unending list of cases pending in the three subordinate courts. Worse, a single day's strike in the courts push these cases back by at least four months. But this fails to move the lawyers. In Delhi they have already struck work 14 times in 1994. Over 4.47 lakh cases are pending in the three subordinate court premises at Tis Hazari, Shahadra and Patiala House, an astounding figure which speaks volumes on the disposal of cases. Cases filed almost three decades ago are still hanging fire causing untold miseries to the litigants.

The majority of the lawyers are not knowledgeable enough to understand the case in its proper perspective and to put forth the finer points of law. They try to make up for this inefficiency by resorting to gimmickry with the sole aim of impressing the clients. Professional ethics is going to winds.

The tenor of arguments in the courts is shifting more towards tackling the witness rather than tackling the facts and the law. Delay and extraneous pressures are used to dissuade a witness. It is easy to attack the character of women victims on frivolous grounds. Professional dishonesty is climbing up to new heights.

The Role of the Judges

The judges and magistrates are more interested in completing their quota of cases on which their future and promotions depended. The number of cases to be tried ran in thousands so the question of concern for the victim did not arise. 'Why should we be the knights in the shining armour when the apex court and the Government did nothing to alleviate the situation and to clear the back log?' 'Instead of appointing judges to fill vacancies they appoint Committees to know the facts which are already known,' said one of the Sessions Judge.

Mostly the judges select few simple cases that they intend to decide, for the rest of the cases, court peons and other officials are asked to give new dates, this was a very common practice. Judges and Magistrates were not even concerned about urgent cases for which the time frame was given in the legal enactments or the rules framed thereunder. 'There are thousands of such urgent cases what can we do? We are not super humans,' was the stock reply.

At higher level every Bench is supposed to work for five hours but a common practice of judges rising up early for want of work was noticed.... this would shock anyone's conscience particularly those who are aware of such heavy arrears pending. There is no proper method of utilising the man-hours by way of proper distribution of work. The general complaint of the litigants was, 'though the cases are noted for hearing they are not heard for days or weeks together, very often special dates are given only to be changed as the court had no time to take up the case,' maintaining time schedule proved to be the most ticklish problem.

A review of the cases decided by the hierarchy of courts uncovers the divergent decision of the Supreme Court and the High Courts on the same issue. The overruling of cases on appeal was quite frequent.

There were several judges whose socio-legal values leave much to be desired. They decided cases of crimes against women in the most conservative manner. Divergent and clashing social orientation of the Supreme Court was alarming. Cases showing insensitivity of the judges to rape and dowry victims was distressing.

Role of Public Interest Litigation

A positive development in the form of Public Interest Litigation (PIL) showing judicial involvement in the social, political and economic affairs of the society through legal activism of the judges was seen in some cases involving women where woman service was rendered to the cause of the suffering women by the simple and speedy dispensation of justice. In *Gaurav Jain* v. *Union of India,* Visaljeet had exposed the miserable plight of the women who were languishing in the brothels. He had brought to the notice of the court the fact that prostitution had become a highly organised industry and requested the court to appoint a commission to go into the various details of this evil and take steps to curb it. In *Bholanath Tripathi* v. *State of UP* a journalist had brought out the plight of Kanchan Devi. The husband had married her and given Rs. 45,000 to her parents. She was held in confinement and used by the husband for earning selling her body.

The Supreme Court deprecated the inordinate delay in listing an important PIL. A Commission was appointed to get the statement of the victim to ensure the authenticity of this *prima facie* case, and arrangements were made for adequate police protection.

PIL is a very positive development. It gives an opportunity to public minded persons to rise up to the occasion and help women in distress. Even destitute women who have no other means of getting justice can dream of getting quick justice. They can seek the indulgence of the court through PIL and get the benefit of protective legislation. Though the Chief Justice of India commands a nationwide network of officially funded network of legal aid through the Committee for the Implementation of Legal Aid Schemes and State Legal Aid Boards, yet none of them has a full time duty lawyer to ensure the basic rights of women and children.

Judicial silence unfortunately exists even though under the legal aid rules of the apex court, its parallel Public Interest Litigation Cell and the Chief Justice of High Courts have power to direct the filing of a case in any such matter.

The legal aid programmes has helped only a fringe of litigants.

Corruption

Corruption of different intensities was found in the whole of the enforcement machinery. Earlier judiciary was a competent organisation having a large number of honest people and corruption was a problem at the lower level but today charges involve even those at the higher rung. This phenomenon may be due to the general decline in allegiance to the moral values of the society, "no one can remain immune to it, still those manning the judiciary, because of their special role, have to project an image of being unbiased, with higher standards of rectitude and integrity" was the consensus of those who were questioned. One possible reason that came out was the fact that the appointment and transfers of judges are not made on the basis of the norm of merit-cum-seniority.

Corruption was in existence at each level of the enforcement machinery, amongst the police, advocates, court officials and the jail machinery, amongst the police, advocates, court officials and the jail authorities, the difference was only of degrees. Bribe was a regular business. If the offender was prepared to oblige the police, the woman would have to run from pillar to post, just to get her case registered, even then there is no surety about the outcome. There were innumerable cases when the Supreme Court had to intervene and ask the SPs how they had closed cases of heinous crimes even of dowry deaths as mere accidents, or cases of rapes and prostitution as non-existent. Several cases of eve teasing indulged in by policemen, which were not registered by their colleagues, came to light. Cases of police brutality and costodial rape were seen to be mounting.

There were several instances of close relatives of judges practicing in the same court and there were proofs of a deplorable practice of judges cultivating politicians for individual gains. High cost of litigation because of delays and corruption was a very disturbing feature. It had a very demoralising effect on women.

The Courts are not always impartial nor are judgements given on merit. A pro-rich bias was clearly visible. For some rich litigants the judges can sit in the chamber beyond working hours and give a decision, while for the poor litigants paucity of time is the reason to prolong the case. The poor litigants may keep running from pillar to post to get the process hurried up or even for directions to be issued to the police or the CID to start investigations or initiate legal proceedings.

An analysis of the convictions for crimes shows that very few rich people get convicted; not that the rich do not commit crimes but their apprehension and conviction is not an easy task. The offenders who were interviewed had the same feeling, they were convinced that with money anything can be brought, even acquittals were not difficult with money power.

The rules of legal enactments direct that the investigation of serious crimes should be done by an officer not below the rank of the Assistant Commissioner of Police (ACP) and it should be reviewed by the Deputy Commissioner of Police (DCP) regularly. further it states that the investigation should not be closed without the prior appraisal of the ACP and the progress made in investigation of such cases should be regularly reviewed by the Police Commissioner every week. The DCP and the ACP are required to visit the scene of the crime on receipt of the information of bride burning or death in unnatural circumstances. They must personally satisfy themselves about the nature of the evidence. But these stipulations are never adhered to. The DCP and the ACP routinely affix their signature to the investigation done by a junior police officer without even bothering to check the work done by him or to guide in his job.

Judicial System Apathetic to the Victims

On 13 March 1992 Delhi High Court acquitted a man charged with burning his wife to death in 1984. He was acquitted because "before the deceased could make a statement to the doctor, her mother had reached the hospital so the possibility of tutoring could not be ruled out!" In another case in March 1992 the Supreme Court reduced the sentence of the accused in a case of rape on a minor while disposing of an appeal from the Madhya Pradesh Government after nine years pendency in the apex court. The trial court had convicted the accused but the High Court did not find cogent evidence about the identity of the accused and acquitted him. Holding that a girl could not have forgotten the face of the man who had committed such a ghastly crime and agreeing with the trial court that the accused was guilty of rape, the Supreme Court just reduced the sentence to the period already undergone. No other reason was given for the reduction of sentence for this inhuman crime.

In the gruesome crime of bride burning Shalini Malhotra, had held her husband responsible for setting her on fire, in a (video taped) dying statement to the Doordarshan years ago in 1989, yet her husband managed to get a bail.

This case which had created such public outcry and stirred the conscience of the nation is till dragging in the court and is only in the initial stage. Woman's organisations and other knowledgeable persons feel that the law not be able to reach the culprit because he is wealthy and influential. The feeling of being defeated by a heartless legal system was writ large on the face of parents who were interviewed, they were greatly disturbed by the news that this offender, who is under trial, is remarried and is not worried about the case.

There were many cases which clearly showed lack of sensitivity on the part of the judges, magistrates and the lawyers. They do nothing to ensure that justice is dispensed speedily. Dates for hearing of cases are announced but they are ignored with impunity by the offenders. The case drags on in spite of repeated entreaties by the victims for a speedy trial. Even those cases which should be speedily disposed of, take years to be decided.

The guidelines provided by the legislature for speedy disposal of cases are normally not adhered to. According to Section 21-B of the Hindu Marriage Act every appeal under the Act is required to be heard as expeditiously as possible, with an endeavour to conclude the hearing within three months from the date of serving of notice on the respondent, but even the apex court sidelines this stipulation. All the enforcement agencies seem to contribute in delaying the trial and creating hurdles for the victim to get justice. Cases drag on for years with no feelings for the difficulties for the indigent and harassed wife.

The Dowry Act provides for the appointment of dowry prohibition officers but till date these Dowry Prohibition Officers have not coordinated their efforts with the police and the Deputy Commissioner Police Ms. Hazarika who is in charge of the Crimes (Women) Cell, was not even aware that any such regulation exists. She had to dig out these regulations from the old files to find out about the appointment of these officers.

The law-makers had recognised the role of social workers in 1986. Delhi police has appointed 28 social workers from different organisations 'to recommend the cases of women.' This was done to give voluntary agencies a chance to play a greater role in rooting out crimes against women as envisaged in the amended Acts. "But their work has not matched our expectations," said a senior police officer.

"There was time," said another police officer, "when a single case of bride burning would spark off protests, demonstrations or at least letters to the editors. That was in late seventies and early eighties, now so many dowry deaths go unnoticed without any protest."

Similar are the counter charges by members of the voluntary groups. They say that police action falls short of their expectations. Social workers are working on dowry cases without the punch that Dowry Act and the cooperation of the police can give them.

The judges blame lawyers for bench hunting and pleading for adjournments on frivolous grounds wasting the time of the courts and other litigants. The advocates and the police blame the judiciary for the dilatory process of justice and for insisting too much on evidence.

Criminalisation of Politics

It makes a mockery of protective laws. Bharti Narula was burnt by her in-laws and people demonstrated at their residence in Gulmohar Park. The culprits sold off their house and shifted somewhere else. Meanwhile the eye witnesses of the case, a woman and her three daughters received threats and turned hostile. Such was the clout of the accused that the SHO of the area was transferred.

It was told by several persons that the SHO was convinced of the genuineness of the case and was keen to pursue it, this led to his transfer. The court, predictably, ruled that the police had failed to make out a case. It ignored all the circumstantial evidence.

Dishonest and incompetent officers, who are prepared to collaborate with ministerial corruption are often put in key position and honest and efficient officer sidelined. There were several police personnel, who are downright dishonest, corrupt, inefficient and supine, they were in Delhi for years. In recent years, the standard of the police force has fallen and discipline had has also gone down. The judiciary has not remained totally untouched. There were corrupt judges, several vacancies are not filled due to political wrangles, and transfers of judges are politicised.

Crimes (Women) Cell

In October 1986 Crimes (women) Cell came into existence. It replaced Anti-dowry Cell created in 1983 as an experiment to give relief to the growing number of battered, abandoned and terror striken wives. Surprisingly, no specific guidelines were framed for this very Special Cell. It was given neither new powers nor any observable autonomy. However, a full cadre was created for the Cell but none of the appointees had neither special credentials for the job nor they had received any special training for it. "We have tried to keep honest and clean officers with the right attitude," explained the Deputy Commissioner Police (DCP) Mrs. Mehra. In 1991, a specialised counselling service by trained psychologists was introduced but due to the large number of cases and shortage of time the work of the counsellors was not very impressive.

There is a growth in the number of complaints registered in the Cell yet compromises, convictions and cases filed in courts by it has declined. Even the compromised cases are statistically unreliable. 60% of the 20 compromised cases examined during an investigation, had never received any follow up call from the Cell, about 20% had broken up but the Cell was not even aware of them. The aggrieved women were so disgusted and disillusioned with the lack of concern of the officers of the Cell to find out about their welfare.

Legal Aid Cells

Legal aid cells is another positive development. It is felt that these Cells, if they work with dedication and sincerity, can do a lot of good in making women aware of their rights and competent enough to fight for their rights. The Delhi Legal Aid Cell has branches in Patiala House, Tees Hazari Courts, the High Court and the Supreme Court. They provide women with lawyers to fight their cases and give legal aid to those who seek assistance either directly or through the PIL.

The National Committee for the Implementation of Legal Aid recognised the fact that women have been subjected to deprivation, brutality and exploitation for such a long time that they cannot stand on their feet. It has suggested initiation of programmes for training women social workers in the use of law on all women subjects. It has also evolved a model scheme under which all women irrespective of their economic status are entitled to free legal aid. This would help economically handicapped women, to fight for their right.

Family Courts and Lok Adalats

Family Courts Act was passed in 1984 with an aim to make the legal process less technical and speedier. Most of the family matters were expected to be transferred to these courts from the regular courts, but the implementation of this Act has not been very encouraging only few States have established these courts. In Delhi vested interests prevented the implementation of this Act. There was a lawyer's strike to protest the establishment of Family Courts, consequently there are no family courts in Delhi.

Lok Adalats are doing their bit in taking the load off the regular courts. But the efforts to organise these adalats and the procedure of transferring cases from the regular courts has not brought any appreciable decline in the number of pending cases in the regular courts. Surprisingly the Family Courts or Lok Adalats have not shown much popularity with the litigants.

Women's Organisations

There has been a proliferation of women's groups in the last fifteen years. Most of these groups were initially set up in response to the increasing atrocities on women, specially cruelty in marriage. In the earlier years of their existence these organisations responded to these gruesome killings by organising protest demonstrations against the families where the crimes took place as well as against the inefficient Government machinery including the police which went out of their way to project these murders as accidents or suicides. Gradually, these organisations began to feel that it was useless to protest after the woman has died so they should try to save the woman while she was still alive. Beginning in the early 1980s, women's group tried to meet the challenge by setting up legal aid and support groups for women in distress. They hoped that by offering timely support and help, they would be able to encourage women to resist maltreatment and to walk out of a violent or oppressive family situations before they could be killed or driven to commit suicide.

These groups have tackled some of the real issues like rape, eve teasing, prostitution and dowry, etc. They have been given crucial role in legal aid schemes concerning welfare and emancipation of women. The efforts on the part of these organisations to educate the women in their legal rights have, however, not been adequate and a lot more needs to be done. In Delhi about 30 cases of dowry deaths are being taken up by these women's organisations to ensure the conviction of the accused. These women's organisations have held demonstrations a number of times against certain court judgments and filed review petitions in the apex court to get justice for their clients.

Legal System is a Reflection of the Society

Improved laws can have little impact upon the cultural values of the society unless the society adopts the new values and integrates them in its institutions. It is a process of action, reaction and interaction between the legal system and the cultural attitudes. When the society itself is becoming criminal and escapist how can we expect its members to behave differently? The legal system is only reflecting the chaos and aggression in the society, its acquisitive urges and the degeneration of values.

One of the causes of the increasing crimes against women seems to be the superimposition of the developmental programmes on the pre-existing system which is severely biased against women. The developmental planning, being male biased has not been conducive to the creation of the much needed ideological and institutional changes. The reason is the inability of both, men and women, to adjust themselves to the new changes, which have resulted in frustration, dissatisfaction and the increasing number of criminal acts. In order to be successfully eliminated these crimes should be understood in the frame work of the larger social and familial structures that nurture these exploitative relations

Role of the Media

Investigative journalism, exposure of crimes through radio, TV and the general interest magazines has gone a long way in shaking up the enforcement agencies into action and inspired them to do a bit of introspection and to work towards more effective implementation of the laws meant to ameliorate the condition of women. Media has also played a role in educating the masses about their legal rights but a lot more needs to be done.

Resistance to Crimes has Broken Down

It was observed that people in general have become very materialistic. The informal restraints of values like truth, honesty, morality, etc., have disappeared in the rat race of individual fulfilment. Human beings have become too demanding and have lost the finer sentiments of compassion, mercy and consideration for others. The in-built controls on the individual which used to be drilled in childhood by parents and friends have disappeared. Children grope for values, they are like a rudderless ship. They get misguided. Fighting between parents, daughters-in-law and the mother-in-law, the prevailing corruption and the high place of money in society, all have their impact. The attitude of women has also changed, they are no longer prepared to patch up and the man is not willing to relent from his feudal ideas, forgetting that compromise and adjustment is the basis of any bilateral relation.

In spite of a large number of conferences and workshops

conducted by the National Council for Social Defence and the Ministry of Human Resources and the efforts of Women's Organisations there has been very little systematic, coordinated and planned efforts, either to understand criminal behaviour in its varied dimensions or to evolve appropriate strategies to make institutional arrangements to meet the challenge of these crimes and plan out strategies for the effective enforcement of laws. The knowledge available as a reuslt of the developments in behavioural sciences as well as physical and natural sciences does not appear to have made any impact on the policies of social defence. The criminal justice system continues to operate on doubtful presumptions and archaic procedures. Crimes against women keep repeating themselves like history. They have become so normal that peoples' conscience is not stirred by their frequent recurrence. In fact, incident of these crimes is not as shocking as their easy acceptance by the society.

The law in action is totally different from the law in books and the existing legal provisions have not been effective in arresting the increasing number of crimes against women.

Despite all efforts and idealism, the protective laws do not protect. As an institution, laws reflect the power structure of our society and are subject to the same prejudices and bias against women as the society is. Law is basically a set of power resources, it is a tool in the hands of the stronger section of the population to have their way, with a semblance of being just and charitable to the weaker sections of the society.

Incidents of dowry deaths, cruelty, rape, prostitution, bigamy and other heinous crimes against women have been regularly reported by the press and the media and have been high lighted by the women's organisations since eighties yet even the apex court has not done anything in its role as prime guardian of life of the citizens. Probably, it is only the judiciary led by the Supreme Court which can possibly remedy the prevailing dismal situation.

The Supreme Court has propounded in elevating phrases a whole bundle of rights of a life with dignity, out of the life and liberty right. But even the right of survival of the most protected citizens under the Constitution, does not get priority of the court's time. Cases punishable with life imprisonment have been kept pending for more than 12 years even in the highest court. *Suo motu* notice of newspaper reports is taken of the death of the rich and the influential like the case of Sawinder Singh and Thapars who were involved in economic offences but nothing is done when newspapers report cases of the most brutal cases of dowry death or rape which cannot be registered because the victim is poor or there is resistance from the enforcement authorities.

5

Optional Protocol to the Convention on the Elimination of Discrimination against Women, 2000

G.A. Res. 54/4, annex, 54 U.N. GAOR Supp. (No. 49) at 5, U.N. Doc. A/54/49 (Vol. I) (2000), entered into force Dec. 22, 2000.

The States Parties to the present Protocol,

Noting that the Charter of the United Nations reaffirms faith in fundamental human rights, in the dignity and worth of the human person and in the equal rights of men and women,

Also noting that the Universal Declaration of Human Rights Resolution 217 A (III). proclaims that all human beings are born free and equal in dignity and rights and that everyone is entitled to all the rights and freedoms set forth therein, without distinction of any kind, including distinction based on sex,

Recalling that the International Covenants on Human Rights Resolution 2200 A (XXI), annex. and other international human rights instruments prohibit discrimination on the basis of sex,

Also recalling the Convention on the Elimination of All Forms of Discrimination against Women4 ("the Convention"), in which the States Parties thereto condemn discrimination against women in all its forms and agree to pursue by all appropriate means and without delay a policy of eliminating discrimination against women,

Reaffirming their determination to ensure the full and equal enjoyment by women of all human rights and fundamental freedoms and to take effective action to prevent violations of these rights and freedoms,

Have agreed as follows:

Article 1

A State Party to the present Protocol ("State Party") recognizes the competence of the Committee on the Elimination of Discrimination against Women ("the Committee") to receive and consider communications submitted in accordance with article 2.

Article 2

Communications may be submitted by or on behalf of individuals or groups of individuals, under the jurisdiction of a State Party, claiming to be victims of a violation of any of the rights set forth in the Convention by that State Party. Where a communication is submitted on behalf of individuals or groups of individuals, this shall be with their consent unless the author can justify acting on their behalf without such consent.

Article 3

Communications shall be in writing and shall not be anonymous. No communication shall be received by the Committee if it concerns a State Party to the Convention that is not a party to the present Protocol.

Article 4

1. The Committee shall not consider a communication unless it has ascertained that all available domestic remedies have been exhausted unless the application of such remedies is unreasonably prolonged or unlikely to bring effective relief.

2. The Committee shall declare a communication inadmissible where:

(a) The same matter has already been examined by the Committee or has been or is being examined under another procedure of international investigation or settlement;

(b) It is incompatible with the provisions of the Convention;

(c) It is manifestly ill-founded or not sufficiently substantiated;

(d) It is an abuse of the right to submit a communication;

(e) The facts that are the subject of the communication occurred prior to the entry into force of the present Protocol for the State Party concerned unless those facts continued after that date.

Article 5

1. At any time after the receipt of a communication and before a determination on the merits has been reached, the Committee may transmit to the State Party concerned for its urgent consideration a request that the State Party take such interim measures as may be necessary to avoid possible irreparable damage to the victim or victims of the alleged violation.

2. Where the Committee exercises its discretion under

paragraph 1 of the present article, this does not imply a determination on admissibility or on the merits of the communication.

Article 6

1. Unless the Committee considers a communication inadmissible without reference to the State Party concerned, and provided that the individual or individuals consent to the disclosure of their identity to that State Party, the Committee shall bring any communication submitted to it under the present Protocol confidentially to the attention of the State Party concerned.

2. Within six months, the receiving State Party shall submit to the Committee written explanations or statements clarifying the matter and the remedy, if any, that may have been provided by that State Party.

Article 7

1. The Committee shall consider communications received under the present Protocol in the light of all information made available to it by or on behalf of individuals or groups of individuals and by the State Party concerned, provided that this information is transmitted to the parties concerned.

2. The Committee shall hold closed meetings when examining communications under the present Protocol.

3. After examining a communication, the Committee shall transmit its views on the communication, together with its recommendations, if any, to the parties concerned.

4. The State Party shall give due consideration to the views of the Committee, together with its recommendations, if any, and shall submit to the Committee, within six

months, a written response, including information on any action taken in the light of the views and recommendations of the Committee.

5. The Committee may invite the State Party to submit further information about any measures the State Party has taken in response to its views or recommendations, if any, including as deemed appropriate by the Committee, in the State Party's subsequent reports under article 18 of the Convention.

Article 8

1. If the Committee receives reliable information indicating grave or systematic violations by a State Party of rights set forth in the Convention, the Committee shall invite that State Party to cooperate in the examination of the information and to this end to submit observations with regard to the information concerned.

2. Taking into account any observations that may have been submitted by the State Party concerned as well as any other reliable information available to it, the Committee may designate one or more of its members to conduct an inquiry and to report urgently to the Committee. Where warranted and with the consent of the State Party, the inquiry may include a visit to its territory.

3. After examining the findings of such an inquiry, the Committee shall transmit these findings to the State Party concerned together with any comments and recommendations.

4. The State Party concerned shall, within six months of receiving the findings, comments and recommendations transmitted by the Committee, submit its observations to the Committee.

5. Such an inquiry shall be conducted confidentially and the cooperation of the State Party shall be sought at all stages of the proceedings.

Article 9

1. The Committee may invite the State Party concerned to include in its report under article 18 of the Convention details of any measures taken in response to an inquiry conducted under article 8 of the present Protocol.

2. The Committee may, if necessary, after the end of the period of six months referred to in article 8.4, invite the State Party concerned to inform it of the measures taken in response to such an inquiry.

Article 10

1. Each State Party may, at the time of signature or ratification of the present Protocol or accession thereto, declare that it does not recognize the competence of the Committee provided for in articles 8 and 9.

2. Any State Party having made a declaration in accordance with paragraph 1 of the present article may, at any time, withdraw this declaration by notification to the Secretary-General.

Article 11

A State Party shall take all appropriate steps to ensure that individuals under its jurisdiction are not subjected to ill treatment or intimidation as a consequence of communicating with the Committee pursuant to the present Protocol.

Article 12

The Committee shall include in its annual report under

article 21 of the Convention a summary of its activities under the present Protocol.

Article 13

Each State Party undertakes to make widely known and to give publicity to the Convention and the present Protocol and to facilitate access to information about the views and recommendations of the Committee, in particular, on matters involving that State Party.

Article 14

The Committee shall develop its own rules of procedure to be followed when exercising the functions conferred on it by the present Protocol.

Article 15

1. The present Protocol shall be open for signature by any State that has signed, ratified or acceded to the Convention.

2. The present Protocol shall be subject to ratification by any State that has ratified or acceded to the Convention. Instruments of ratification shall be deposited with the Secretary-General of the United Nations.

3. The present Protocol shall be open to accession by any State that has ratified or acceded to the Convention.

4. Accession shall be effected by the deposit of an instrument of accession with the Secretary-General of the United Nations.

Article 16

1. The present Protocol shall enter into force three months after the date of the deposit with the Secretary-

General of the United Nations of the tenth instrument of ratification or accession.

2. For each State ratifying the present Protocol or acceding to it after its entry into force, the present Protocol shall enter into force three months after the date of the deposit of its own instrument of ratification or accession.

Article 17

No reservations to the present Protocol shall be permitted.

Article 18

1. Any State Party may propose an amendment to the present Protocol and file it with the Secretary-General of the United Nations. The Secretary-General shall thereupon communicate any proposed amendments to the States Parties with a request that they notify her or him whether they favour a conference of States Parties for the purpose of considering and voting on the proposal. In the event that at least one third of the States Parties favour such a conference, the Secretary-General shall convene the conference under the auspices of the United Nations. Any amendment adopted by a majority of the States Parties present and voting at the conference shall be submitted to the General Assembly of the United Nations for approval.

2. Amendments shall come into force when they have been approved by the General Assembly of the United Nations and accepted by a two-thirds majority of the States Parties to the present Protocol in accordance with their respective constitutional processes.

3. When amendments come into force, they shall be binding on those States Parties that have accepted them, other States Parties still being bound by the provisions of

the present Protocol and any earlier amendments that they have accepted.

Article 19

1. Any State Party may denounce the present Protocol at any time by written notification addressed to the Secretary-General of the United Nations. Denunciation shall take effect six months after the date of receipt of the notification by the Secretary-General.

2. Denunciation shall be without prejudice to the continued application of the provisions of the present Protocol to any communication submitted under article 2 or any inquiry initiated under article 8 before the effective date of denunciation.

Article 20

The Secretary-General of the United Nations shall inform all States of:

(a) Signatures, ratifications and accessions under the present Protocol;

(b) The date of entry into force of the present Protocol and of any amendment under article 18;

(c) Any denunciation under article 19.

Article 21

1. The present Protocol, of which the Arabic, Chinese, English, French, Russian and Spanish texts are equally authentic, shall be deposited in the archives of the United Nations.

2. The Secretary-General of the United Nations shall transmit certified copies of the present Protocol to all States referred to in article 25 of the Convention.

6

Declaration on the Elimination of Violence against Women, 1993

G.A. res. 48/104, 48 U.N. GAOR Supp. (No. 49) at 217, U.N. Doc. A/48/49 (1993)

The General Assembly,

Recognizing the urgent need for the universal application to women of the rights and principles with regard to equality, security, liberty, integrity and dignity of all human beings,

Noting that those rights and principles are enshrined in international instruments, including the Universal Declaration of Human Rights, the International Covenant on Civil and Political Rights, the International Covenant on Economic, Social and Cultural Rights, the Convention on the Elimination of All Forms of Discrimination against Women and the Convention against Torture and Other Cruel, Inhuman or Degrading Treatment or Punishment,

Recognizing that effective implementation of the Convention on the Elimination of All Forms of Discrimination against Women would contribute to the elimination of violence against women and that the Declaration on the Elimination of Violence against Women, set forth in the present resolution, will strengthen and complement that process,

Concerned that violence against women is an obstacle to the achievement of equality, development and peace, as recognized in the Nairobi Forward-looking Strategies for the Advancement of Women, in which a set of measures to combat violence against women was recommended, and to the full implementation of the Convention on the Elimination of All Forms of Discrimination against Women,

Affirming that violence against women constitutes a violation of the rights and fundamental freedoms of women and impairs or nullifies their enjoyment of those rights and freedoms, and concerned about the long-standing failure to protect and promote those rights and freedoms in the case of violence against women,

Recognizing that violence against women is a manifestation of historically unequal power relations between men and women, which have led to domination over and discrimination against women by men and to the prevention of the full advancement of women, and that violence against women is one of the crucial social mechanisms by which women are forced into a subordinate position compared with men,

Concerned that some groups of women, such as women belonging to minority groups, indigenous women, refugee women, migrant women, women living in rural or remote communities, destitute women, women in institutions or in detention, female children, women with disabilities, elderly women and women in situations of armed conflict, are especially vulnerable to violence,

Recalling the conclusion in paragraph 23 of the annex

to Economic and Social Council resolution 1990/15 of 24 May 1990 that the recognition that violence against women in the family and society was pervasive and cut across lines of income, class and culture had to be matched by urgent and effective steps to eliminate its incidence,

Recalling also Economic and Social Council resolution 1991/18 of 30 May 1991, in which the Council recommended the development of a framework for an international instrument that would address explicitly the issue of violence against women,

Welcoming the role that women's movements are playing in drawing increasing attention to the nature, severity and magnitude of the problem of violence against women,

Alarmed that opportunities for women to achieve legal, social, political and economic equality in society are limited, inter alia, by continuing and endemic violence,

Convinced that in the light of the above there is a need for a clear and comprehensive definition of violence against women, a clear statement of the rights to be applied to ensure the elimination of violence against women in all its forms, a commitment by States in respect of their responsibilities, and a commitment by the international community at large to the elimination of violence against women,

Solemnly proclaims the following Declaration on the Elimination of Violence against Women and urges that every effort be made so that it becomes generally known and respected:

Article 1

For the purposes of this Declaration, the term "violence against women" means any act of gender-based violence that results in, or is likely to result in, physical, sexual or psychological harm or suffering to women, including threats of such acts, coercion or arbitrary deprivation of liberty, whether occurring in public or in private life.

Article 2

Violence against women shall be understood to encompass, but not be limited to, the following:

(a) Physical, sexual and psychological violence occurring in the family, including battering, sexual abuse of female children in the household, dowry-related violence, marital rape, female genital mutilation and other traditional practices harmful to women, non-spousal violence and violence related to exploitation;

(b) Physical, sexual and psychological violence occurring within the general community, including rape, sexual abuse, sexual harassment and intimidation at work, in educational institutions and elsewhere, trafficking in women and forced prostitution;

(c) Physical, sexual and psychological violence perpetrated or condoned by the State, wherever it occurs.

Article 3

Women are entitled to the equal enjoyment and protection of all human rights and fundamental freedoms in the political, economic, social, cultural, civil or any other field. These rights include, inter alia:

(a) The right to life;

(b) The right to equality;

(c) The right to liberty and security of person;

(d) The right to equal protection under the law;

(e) The right to be free from all forms of discrimination;

(f) The right to the highest standard attainable of physical and mental health;

(g) The right to just and favourable conditions of work;

(h) The right not to be subjected to torture, or other cruel, inhuman or degrading treatment or punishment.

Article 4

States should condemn violence against women and should not invoke any custom, tradition or religious consideration to avoid their obligations with respect to its elimination. States should pursue by all appropriate means and without delay a policy of eliminating violence against women and, to this end, should:

(a) Consider, where they have not yet done so, ratifying or acceding to the Convention on the Elimination of All Forms of Discrimination against Women or withdrawing reservations to that Convention;

(b) Refrain from engaging in violence against women;

(c) Exercise due diligence to prevent, investigate and, in accordance with national legislation, punish acts of violence against women, whether those acts are perpetrated by the State or by private persons;

(d) Develop penal, civil, labour and administrative sanctions in domestic legislation to punish and redress the wrongs caused to women who are subjected to violence; women who are subjected to violence should be provided with access to the mechanisms of justice and, as provided for by national legislation, to just and effective remedies for the harm that they have suffered; States should also inform women of their rights in seeking redress through such mechanisms;

(e) Consider the possibility of developing national plans of action to promote the protection of women against any form of violence, or to include provisions for that purpose in plans already existing, taking into account, as appropriate, such cooperation as can be provided by non-governmental organizations, particularly those concerned with the issue of violence against women;

(f) Develop, in a comprehensive way, preventive approaches and all those measures of a legal, political, administrative and cultural nature that promote the protection of women against any form of violence, and ensure that the re-victimization of women does not occur because of laws insensitive to gender considerations, enforcement practices or other interventions;

(g) Work to ensure, to the maximum extent feasible in the light of their available resources and, where needed, within the framework of international cooperation, that women subjected to violence and, where appropriate, their children have specialized assistance, such as rehabilitation, assistance in child care and maintenance, treatment, counselling, and health and social services, facilities and programmes, as well as support structures, and should take all other appropriate measures to promote their safety and physical and psychological rehabilitation;

(h) Include in government budgets adequate resources for their activities related to the elimination of violence against women;

(i) Take measures to ensure that law enforcement officers and public officials responsible for implementing policies to prevent, investigate and punish violence against women receive training to sensitize them to the needs of women;

(j) Adopt all appropriate measures, especially in the field of education, to modify the social and cultural patterns of conduct of men and women and to eliminate prejudices, customary practices and all other practices based on the idea of the inferiority or superiority of either of the sexes and on stereotyped roles for men and women;

(k) Promote research, collect data and compile statistics, especially concerning domestic violence, relating to the prevalence of different forms of violence against women and encourage research on the causes, nature, seriousness and consequences of violence against women and on the effectiveness of measures implemented to prevent and redress violence against women; those statistics and findings of the research will be made public;

(l) Adopt measures directed towards the elimination of violence against women who are especially vulnerable to violence;

(m) Include, in submitting reports as required under relevant human rights instruments of the United Nations, information pertaining to violence against women and measures taken to implement the present Declaration;

(n) Encourage the development of appropriate guidelines to assist in the implementation of the principles set forth in the present Declaration;

(o) Recognize the important role of the women's movement and non-governmental organizations world wide in raising awareness and alleviating the problem of violence against women;

(p) Facilitate and enhance the work of the women's movement and non-governmental organizations and cooperate with them at local, national and regional levels;

(q) Encourage intergovernmental regional organizations of which they are members to include the elimination of violence against women in their programmes, as appropriate.

Article 5

The organs and specialized agencies of the United Nations system should, within their respective fields of competence, contribute to the recognition and realization of the rights and the principles set forth in the present Declaration and, to this end, should, inter alia:

(a) Foster international and regional cooperation with a view to defining regional strategies for combating violence, exchanging experiences and financing programmes relating to the elimination of violence against women;

(b) Promote meetings and seminars with the aim of creating and raising awareness among all persons of the issue of the elimination of violence against women;

(c) Foster coordination and exchange within the United Nations system between human rights treaty bodies to address the issue of violence against women effectively;

(d) Include in analyses prepared by organizations and bodies of the United Nations system of social trends and problems, such as the periodic reports on the world social situation, examination of trends in violence against women;

(e) Encourage coordination between organizations and bodies of the United Nations system to incorporate the issue of violence against women into ongoing programmes, especially with reference to groups of women particularly vulnerable to violence;

(f) Promote the formulation of guidelines or manuals relating to violence against women, taking into account the measures referred to in the present Declaration;

(g) Consider the issue of the elimination of violence against women, as appropriate, in fulfilling their mandates with respect to the implementation of human rights instruments;

(h) Cooperate with non-governmental organizations in addressing the issue of violence against women.

Article 6

Nothing in the present Declaration shall affect any provision that is more conducive to the elimination of violence against women that may be contained in the legislation of a State or in any international convention, treaty or other instrument in force in a State.

7

Convention on the Elimination of All Forms of Discrimination against Women (1981)

G.A. res. 34/180, 34 U.N. GAOR Supp. (No. 46) at 193, U.N. Doc. A/34/46, entered into force Sept. 3, 1981

The States Parties to the present Convention,

Noting that the Charter of the United Nations reaffirms faith in fundamental human rights, in the dignity and worth of the human person and in the equal rights of men and women,

Noting that the Universal Declaration of Human Rights affirms the principle of the inadmissibility of discrimination and proclaims that all human beings are born free and equal in dignity and rights and that everyone is entitled to all the rights and freedoms set forth therein, without distinction of any kind, including distinction based on sex,

Noting that the States Parties to the International Covenants on Human Rights have the obligation to ensure the equal rights of men and women to enjoy all economic, social, cultural, civil and political rights,

Considering the international conventions concluded

under the auspices of the United Nations and the specialized agencies promoting equality of rights of men and women,

Noting also the resolutions, declarations and recommendations adopted by the United Nations and the specialized agencies promoting equality of rights of men and women,

Concerned, however, that despite these various instruments extensive discrimination against women continues to exist,

Recalling that discrimination against women violates the principles of equality of rights and respect for human dignity, is an obstacle to the participation of women, on equal terms with men, in the political, social, economic and cultural life of their countries, hampers the growth of the prosperity of society and the family and makes more difficult the full development of the potentialities of women in the service of their countries and of humanity,

Concerned that in situations of poverty women have the least access to food, health, education, training and opportunities for employment and other needs,

Convinced that the establishment of the new international economic order based on equity and justice will contribute significantly towards the promotion of equality between men and women,

Emphasizing that the eradication of apartheid, all forms of racism, racial discrimination, colonialism, neo-colonialism, aggression, foreign occupation and domination and interference in the internal affairs of States is essential to the full enjoyment of the rights of men and women,

Affirming that the strengthening of international peace

and security, the relaxation of international tension, mutual co-operation among all States irrespective of their social and economic systems, general and complete disarmament, in particular nuclear disarmament under strict and effective international control, the affirmation of the principles of justice, equality and mutual benefit in relations among countries and the realization of the right of peoples under alien and colonial domination and foreign occupation to self-determination and independence, as well as respect for national sovereignty and territorial integrity, will promote social progress and development and as a consequence will contribute to the attainment of full equality between men and women,

Convinced that the full and complete development of a country, the welfare of the world and the cause of peace require the maximum participation of women on equal terms with men in all fields,

Bearing in mind the great contribution of women to the welfare of the family and to the development of society, so far not fully recognized, the social significance of maternity and the role of both parents in the family and in the upbringing of children, and aware that the role of women in procreation should not be a basis for discrimination but that the upbringing of children requires a sharing of responsibility between men and women and society as a whole,

Aware that a change in the traditional role of men as well as the role of women in society and in the family is needed to achieve full equality between men and women,

Determined to implement the principles set forth in the Declaration on the Elimination of Discrimination against Women and, for that purpose, to adopt the measures required for the elimination of such discrimination in all its forms and manifestations,

Have agreed on the following:

PART I

Article 1

For the purposes of the present Convention, the term "discrimination against women" shall mean any distinction, exclusion or restriction made on the basis of sex which has the effect or purpose of impairing or nullifying the recognition, enjoyment or exercise by women, irrespective of their marital status, on a basis of equality of men and women, of human rights and fundamental freedoms in the political, economic, social, cultural, civil or any other field.

Article 2

States Parties condemn discrimination against women in all its forms, agree to pursue by all appropriate means and without delay a policy of eliminating discrimination against women and, to this end, undertake:

(a) To embody the principle of the equality of men and women in their national constitutions or other appropriate legislation if not yet incorporated therein and to ensure, through law and other appropriate means, the practical realization of this principle;

(b) To adopt appropriate legislative and other measures, including sanctions where appropriate, prohibiting all discrimination against women;

(c) To establish legal protection of the rights of women on an equal basis with men and to ensure through competent national tribunals and other public institutions the effective protection of women against any act of discrimination;

(d) To refrain from engaging in any act or practice of discrimination against women and to ensure that public authorities and institutions shall act in conformity with this obligation;

(e) To take all appropriate measures to eliminate discrimination against women by any person, organization or enterprise;

(f) To take all appropriate measures, including legislation, to modify or abolish existing laws, regulations, customs and practices which constitute discrimination against women;

(g) To repeal all national penal provisions which constitute discrimination against women.

Article 3

States Parties shall take in all fields, in particular in the political, social, economic and cultural fields, all appropriate measures, including legislation, to en sure the full development and advancement of women, for the purpose of guaranteeing them the exercise and enjoyment of human rights and fundamental freedoms on a basis of equality with men.

Article 4

1. Adoption by States Parties of temporary special measures aimed at accelerating de facto equality between men and women shall not be considered discrimination as defined in the present Convention, but shall in no way entail as a consequence the maintenance of unequal or separate standards; these measures shall be discontinued when the objectives of equality of opportunity and treatment have been achieved.

2. Adoption by States Parties of special measures, including those measures contained in the present Convention, aimed at protecting maternity shall not be considered discriminatory.

Article 5

States Parties shall take all appropriate measures:

(a) To modify the social and cultural patterns of conduct of men and women, with a view to achieving the elimination of prejudices and customary and all other practices which are based on the idea of the inferiority or the superiority of either of the sexes or on stereotyped roles for men and women;

(b) To ensure that family education includes a proper understanding of maternity as a social function and the recognition of the common responsibility of men and women in the upbringing and development of their children, it being understood that the interest of the children is the primordial consideration in all cases.

Article 6

States Parties shall take all appropriate measures, including legislation, to suppress all forms of traffic in women and exploitation of prostitution of women.

PART II

Article 7

States Parties shall take all appropriate measures to eliminate discrimination against women in the political and public life of the country and, in particular, shall ensure to women, on equal terms with men, the right:

(a) To vote in all elections and public referenda and to be eligible for election to all publicly elected bodies;

(b) To participate in the formulation of government policy and the implementation thereof and to hold public office and perform all public functions at all levels of government;

(c) To participate in non-governmental organizations and associations concerned with the public and political life of the country.

Article 8

States Parties shall take all appropriate measures to ensure to women, on equal terms with men and without any discrimination, the opportunity to represent their Governments at the international level and to participate in the work of international organizations.

Article 9

1. States Parties shall grant women equal rights with men to acquire, change or retain their nationality. They shall ensure in particular that neither marriage to an alien nor change of nationality by the husband during marriage shall automatically change the nationality of the wife, render her stateless or force upon her the nationality of the husband.

2. States Parties shall grant women equal rights with men with respect to the nationality of their children.

PART III

Article 10

States Parties shall take all appropriate measures to eliminate discrimination against women in order to ensure to them equal rights with men in the field of education and in particular to ensure, on a basis of equality of men and women:

(a) The same conditions for career and vocational guidance, for access to studies and for the achievement of diplomas in educational establishments of all categories in rural as well as in urban areas; this equality shall be ensured in pre-school, general, technical, professional and higher technical education, as well as in all types of vocational training;

(b) Access to the same curricula, the same examinations, teaching staff with qualifications of the same standard and school premises and equipment of the same quality;

(c) The elimination of any stereotyped concept of the roles of men and women at all levels and in all forms of education by encouraging coeducation and other types of education which will help to achieve this aim and, in particular, by the revision of textbooks and school programmes and the adaptation of teaching methods;

(d) The same opportunities to benefit from scholarships and other study grants;

(e) The same opportunities for access to programmes of continuing education, including adult and functional literacy programmes, particulary those aimed at reducing, at the earliest possible time, any gap in education existing between men and women;

(f) The reduction of female student drop-out rates and the organization of programmes for girls and women who have left school prematurely;

(g) The same Opportunities to participate actively in sports and physical education;

(h) Access to specific educational information to help to ensure the health and well-being of families, including information and advice on family planning.

Article 11

1. States Parties shall take all appropriate measures to eliminate discrimination against women in the field of employment in order to ensure, on a basis of equality of men and women, the same rights, in particular:

(a) The right to work as an inalienable right of all human beings;

(b) The right to the same employment opportunities, including the application of the same criteria for selection in matters of employment;

(c) The right to free choice of profession and employment, the right to promotion, job security and all benefits and conditions of service and the right to receive vocational training and retraining, including apprenticeships, advanced vocational training and recurrent training;

(d) The right to equal remuneration, including benefits, and to equal treatment in respect of work of equal value, as well as equality of treatment in the evaluation of the quality of work;

(e) The right to social security, particularly in cases of retirement, unemployment, sickness, invalidity and old age and other incapacity to work, as well as the right to paid leave;

(f) The right to protection of health and to safety in working conditions, including the safeguarding of the function of reproduction.

2. In order to prevent discrimination against women on the grounds of marriage or maternity and to ensure their effective right to work, States Parties shall take appropriate measures:

(a) To prohibit, subject to the imposition of sanctions, dismissal on the grounds of pregnancy or of maternity leave and discrimination in dismissals on the basis of marital status;

(b) To introduce maternity leave with pay or with comparable social benefits without loss of former employment, seniority or social allowances;

(c) To encourage the provision of the necessary supporting social services to enable parents to combine family obligations with work responsibilities and participation in public life, in particular through promoting the establishment and development of a network of child-care facilities;

(d) To provide special protection to women during pregnancy in types of work proved to be harmful to them.

3. Protective legislation relating to matters covered in this article shall be reviewed periodically in the light of scientific and technological knowledge and shall be revised, repealed or extended as necessary.

Article 12

1. States Parties shall take all appropriate measures to eliminate discrimination against women in the field of health care in order to ensure, on a basis of equality of men and women, access to health care services, including those related to family planning.

2. Notwithstanding the provisions of paragraph I of

this article, States Parties shall ensure to women appropriate services in connection with pregnancy, confinement and the post-natal period, granting free services where necessary, as well as adequate nutrition during pregnancy and lactation.

Article 13

States Parties shall take all appropriate measures to eliminate discrimination against women in other areas of economic and social life in order to ensure, on a basis of equality of men and women, the same rights, in particular:

(a) The right to family benefits;

(b) The right to bank loans, mortgages and other forms of financial credit;

(c) The right to participate in recreational activities, sports and all aspects of cultural life.

Article 14

1. States Parties shall take into account the particular problems faced by rural women and the significant roles which rural women play in the economic survival of their families, including their work in the non-monetized sectors of the economy, and shall take all appropriate measures to ensure the application of the provisions of the present Convention to women in rural areas.

2. States Parties shall take all appropriate measures to eliminate discrimination against women in rural areas in order to ensure, on a basis of equality of men and women, that they participate in and benefit from rural development and, in particular, shall ensure to such women the right:

(a) To participate in the elaboration and implementation of development planning at all levels;

(b) To have access to adequate health care facilities, including information, counselling and services in family planning;

(c) To benefit directly from social security programmes;

(d) To obtain all types of training and education, formal and non-formal, including that relating to functional literacy, as well as, inter alia, the benefit of all community and extension services, in order to increase their technical proficiency;

(e) To organize self-help groups and co-operatives in order to obtain equal access to economic opportunities through employment or self employment;

(f) To participate in all community activities;

(g) To have access to agricultural credit and loans, marketing facilities, appropriate technology and equal treatment in land and agrarian reform as well as in land resettlement schemes;

(h) To enjoy adequate living conditions, particularly in relation to housing, sanitation, electricity and water supply, transport and communications.

PART IV

Article 15

1. States Parties shall accord to women equality with men before the law.

2. States Parties shall accord to women, in civil matters, a legal capacity identical to that of men and the same opportunities to exercise that capacity. In particular, they shall give women equal rights to conclude contracts and to administer property and shall treat them equally in all stages of procedure in courts and tribunals.

3. States Parties agree that all contracts and all other private instruments of any kind with a legal effect which is directed at restricting the legal capacity of women shall be deemed null and void.

4. States Parties shall accord to men and women the same rights with regard to the law relating to the movement of persons and the freedom to choose their residence and domicile.

Article 16

1. States Parties shall take all appropriate measures to eliminate discrimination against women in all matters relating to marriage and family relations and in particular shall ensure, on a basis of equality of men and women:

(a) The same right to enter into marriage;

(b) The same right freely to choose a spouse and to enter into marriage only with their free and full consent;

(c) The same rights and responsibilities during marriage and at its dissolution;

(d) The same rights and responsibilities as parents, irrespective of their marital status, in matters relating to their children; in all cases the interests of the children shall be paramount;

(e) The same rights to decide freely and responsibly on the number and spacing of their children and to have access to the information, education and means to enable them to exercise these rights;

(f) The same rights and responsibilities with regard to guardianship, wardship, trusteeship and adoption of children, or similar institutions where these concepts exist in national legislation; in all cases the interests of the children shall be paramount;

(g) The same personal rights as husband and wife, including the right to choose a family name, a profession and an occupation;

(h) The same rights for both spouses in respect of the ownership, acquisition, management, administration, enjoyment and disposition of property, whether free of charge or for a valuable consideration.

2. The betrothal and the marriage of a child shall have no legal effect, and all necessary action, including legislation, shall be taken to specify a minimum age for marriage and to make the registration of marriages in an official registry compulsory.

PART V

Article 17

1. For the purpose of considering the progress made in the implementation of the present Convention, there shall be established a Committee on the Elimination of Discrimination against Women (hereinafter referred to as the Committee) consisting, at the time of entry into force of the Convention, of eighteen and, after ratification of or accession to the Convention by the thirty-fifth State Party, of twenty-three experts of high moral standing and competence in the field covered by the Convention. The experts shall be elected by States Parties from among their nationals and shall serve in their personal capacity, consideration being given to equitable geographical distribution and to the representation of the different forms of civilization as well as the principal legal systems.

2. The members of the Committee shall be elected by

secret ballot from a list of persons nominated by States Parties. Each State Party may nominate one person from among its own nationals.

3. The initial election shall be held six months after the date of the entry into force of the present Convention. At least three months before the date of each election the Secretary-General of the United Nations shall address a letter to the States Parties inviting them to submit their nominations within two months. The Secretary-General shall prepare a list in alphabetical order of all persons thus nominated, indicating the States Parties which have nominated them, and shall submit it to the States Parties.

4. Elections of the members of the Committee shall be held at a meeting of States Parties convened by the Secretary-General at United Nations Headquarters. At that meeting, for which two thirds of the States Parties shall constitute a quorum, the persons elected to the Committee shall be those nominees who obtain the largest number of votes and an absolute majority of the votes of the representatives of States Parties present and voting.

5. The members of the Committee shall be elected for a term of four years. However, the terms of nine of the members elected at the first election shall expire at the end of two years; immediately after the first election the names of these nine members shall be chosen by lot by the Chairman of the Committee.

6. The election of the five additional members of the Committee shall be held in accordance with the provisions of paragraphs 2, 3 and 4 of this article, following the thirty-fifth ratification or accession. The terms of two of the additional members elected on this occasion shall expire

at the end of two years, the names of these two members having been chosen by lot by the Chairman of the Committee.

7. For the filling of casual vacancies, the State Party whose expert has ceased to function as a member of the Committee shall appoint another expert from among its nationals, subject to the approval of the Committee.

8. The members of the Committee shall, with the approval of the General Assembly, receive emoluments from United Nations resources on such terms and conditions as the Assembly may decide, having regard to the importance of the Committee's responsibilities.

9. The Secretary-General of the United Nations shall provide the necessary staff and facilities for the effective performance of the functions of the Committee under the present Convention.

Article 18

1. States Parties undertake to submit to the Secretary-General of the United Nations, for consideration by the Committee, a report on the legislative, judicial, administrative or other measures which they have adopted to give effect to the provisions of the present Convention and on the progress made in this respect:

(a) Within one year after the entry into force for the State concerned;

(b) Thereafter at least every four years and further whenever the Committee so requests.

2. Reports may indicate factors and difficulties affecting the degree of fulfilment of obligations under the present Convention.

Article 19

1. The Committee shall adopt its own rules of procedure.

2. The Committee shall elect its officers for a term of two years.

Article 20

1. The Committee shall normally meet for a period of not more than two weeks annually in order to consider the reports submitted in accordance with article 18 of the present Convention.

2. The meetings of the Committee shall normally be held at United Nations Headquarters or at any other convenient place as determined by the Committee.

Article 21

1. The Committee shall, through the Economic and Social Council, report annually to the General Assembly of the United Nations on its activities and may make suggestions and general recommendations based on the examination of reports and information received from the States Parties. Such suggestions and general recommendations shall be included in the report of the Committee together with comments, if any, from States Parties.

2. The Secretary-General of the United Nations shall transmit the reports of the Committee to the Commission on the Status of Women for its information.

Article 22

The specialized agencies shall be entitled to be represented at the consideration of the implementation of such provisions of the present Convention as fall within the scope of their activities. The Committee may invite the specialized agencies to submit reports on the implementation of the Convention in areas falling within the scope of their activities.

PART VI

Article 23

Nothing in the present Convention shall affect any provisions that are more conducive to the achievement of equality between men and women which may be contained:

(a) In the legislation of a State Party; or

(b) In any other international convention, treaty or agreement in force for that State.

Article 24

States Parties undertake to adopt all necessary measures at the national level aimed at achieving the full realization of the rights recognized in the present Convention.

Article 25

1. The present Convention shall be open for signature by all States.

2. The Secretary-General of the United Nations is designated as the depositary of the present Convention.

3. The present Convention is subject to ratification. Instruments of ratification shall be deposited with the Secretary-General of the United Nations.

4. The present Convention shall be open to accession by all States. Accession shall be effected by the deposit of an instrument of accession with the Secretary-General of the United Nations.

Article 26

1. A request for the revision of the present Convention may be made at any time by any State Party by means of a notification in writing addressed to the Secretary-General of the United Nations.

2. The General Assembly of the United Nations shall decide upon the steps, if any, to be taken in respect of such a request.

Article 27

1. The present Convention shall enter into force on the thirtieth day after the date of deposit with the Secretary-General of the United Nations of the twentieth instrument of ratification or accession.

2. For each State ratifying the present Convention or acceding to it after the deposit of the twentieth instrument of ratification or accession, the Convention shall enter into force on the thirtieth day after the date of the deposit of its own instrument of ratification or accession.

Article 28

1. The Secretary-General of the United Nations shall receive and circulate to all States the text of reservations made by States at the time of ratification or accession.

2. A reservation incompatible with the object and purpose of the present Convention shall not be permitted.

3. Reservations may be withdrawn at any time by notification to this effect addressed to the Secretary-General of the United Nations, who shall then inform all States thereof. Such notification shall take effect on the date on which it is received.

Article 29

1. Any dispute between two or more States Parties concerning the interpretation or application of the present Convention which is not settled by negotiation shall, at the request of one of them, be submitted to arbitration. If within six months from the date of the request for arbitration the parties are unable to agree on the organization of the arbitration, any one of those parties may refer the dispute to the International Court of Justice by request in conformity with the Statute of the Court.

2. Each State Party may at the time of signature or ratification of the present Convention or accession thereto declare that it does not consider itself bound by paragraph I of this article. The other States Parties shall not be bound by that paragraph with respect to any State Party which has made such a reservation.

3. Any State Party which has made a reservation in accordance with paragraph 2 of this article may at any time withdraw that reservation by notification to the Secretary-General of the United Nations.

Article 30

The present Convention, the Arabic, Chinese, English, French, Russian and Spanish texts of which are equally authentic, shall be deposited with the Secretary-General of the United Nations.

In witness whereof the undersigned, duly authorized, have signed the present Convention.

8

The National Commission for Women Act (1990)

[No. 20 of 1990] [30th August, 1990]

An Act to constitute a National Commission for Women and to provide for matters connected therewith or incidental thereto.

Be it enacted by parliament in the Forty-fist Year of the Republic of India as follows:

I. PRELIMINARY

1. Short title, extent and commencement

(1) This Act may be called the National Commission for Women Act, 1990.

(2) It extends to the whole of India except the State of Jammu and Kashmir.

(3) It shall come into force on such date as the Central Government may, by notification in the Official Gazette, appoint.

2. Definitions

In this Act, unless the context otherwise requires,

(a) "Commission" means the National Commission for Women constituted under Sections 3;

(b) "Member" means a Member of the Commission and includes the Member-Secretary;

(c) "Prescribed" means prescribed by rules made under this Act.

II. THE NATIONAL COMMISSION FOR WOMEN

3. Constitution of the National Commission for Women

(1) The Central Government shall constitute a body to be known as the National Commission for Women to exercise the powers conferred on, and to perform the functions assigned to it under this Act.

(2) The Commission shall consist of—

(a) a chairperson, committed to the cause of women, to be nominated by the Central Government;

(b) five Members to be nominated by the Central Government from amongst persons of ability, integrity and standing who have had experience in law or legislation, trade unionism, management of an industry or organization committed to increasing the employment potential of women, women's voluntary organizations (including women activists), administration, economic development, health, education or social welfare:

Provided that at least one Member each shall be from amongst persons belonging to the Scheduled Castes and Scheduled Tribes respectively;

(c) a Member-Secretary to be nominated by the Central Government, who shall be—

(i) an expert in the field of management, organizational structure or sociological movement, or

(ii) an officer who is member of a civil service of the Union or of an all-India service or holds a civil post under the Union with appropriate experience.

4. Term of Office and Conditions of Service of Chairperson and Members

(1) The Chairperson and every Member shall hold office for such period, not exceeding three years, as may be specified by the Central Government in this behalf.

(2) The Chairperson or a Member (other than the Member-Secretary who is a member of a civil service of the Union or of an all-India service or holds a civil post under the Union) may be writing and addressed to the Central Government, resign from the office of Chairperson or, as the case may be of the member at any time.

(3) The Central Government shall remove a person from the office of Chairperson or Member referred to in sub-section (2) if that person—

(a) becomes an undischarged insolvent;

(b) gets convicted and sentenced to imprisonment for an offense which in the opinion of the Central Government involves moral turpitude;

(c) becomes of unsound mind and stands so declared by a competent court;

(d) refuses to act or becomes incapable of acting;

(e) is, without obtaining leave of absence from the Commission, absent from three consecutive meetings of the Commission; or

(f) in the opinion of the Central Government has so abused the position of Chairperson or Member as to render that person's continuance in office detrimental to the public interest;

Provided that no person shall be removed under this clause until that person has been given a reasonable opportunity of being heard in the matter.

(4) A vacancy caused under sub-section (2) or otherwise shall be filled by fresh nomination.

(5) The salaries and allowances payable to and the other terms and conditions of service of the Chairperson and Members shall be such as may be prescribed.

5. Officers and Other Employees of the Commissions

(1) The Central Government shall provide the Commission with such officers and employees as may be necessary for the efficient performance of the functions of the Commission under this Act.

(2) The salaries and allowances payable to, and the other terms and conditions of service of the officers and other employees appointed for the purpose of the Commission shall be such as may be prescribed.

6. Salaries and Allowances to be Paid out of Grants

The salaries and allowances payable to the Chairperson and Members and the administrative expenses, including salaries, allowances and pensions payable to the officers and other employees referred to in Section 5 shall be paid out of the grants referred to in sub-section (1) of Section 11.

7. Vacancies, etc., Not to Invalidate Proceeding of the Commission

No act or proceeding of the Commission shall be questioned or shall be invalid on the ground merely of the existence of any vacancy of defect in the constitution of the Commission.

8. Committees of the Commission

(1) The Commission may appoint such Committees as may be necessary for dealing with such special issues as may be taken up by the Commission from time to time.

(2) The Commission shall have the power to co-opt as members of any committee appointed under sub-section (1) such number of persons, who are not Members of the Commission, as it may think fit and the persons so co-opted shall have the right to attend the meetings of the committee and take part in its proceedings but shall not have the right to vote.

(3) The person so co-opted shall be entitled to receive such allowances for attending the meetings of the Committee as may be prescribed.

9. Procedure to be Regulated by the Commission

(1) The Commission or a committee thereof shall meet as and when necessary and shall meet at such time and place as the Chairperson may think fit.

(2) The Commission shall regulate its own procedure of the committees thereof.

(3) All orders and decisions of the Commission shall be authenticated by the Member-Secretary or any other of the Commission duly authorised by the Member-Secretary in this behalf.

9

The Commission of SATI (Prevention) Act (1987)

(No. 3of 1988)

An Act to provide for the more effective prevention of the commission of sati and its glorification and for matters connected therewith or incidental thereto.

Whereas *sati* or the burning or burying alive of widows or women is revolting to the feelings of human nature and nowhere enjoined by any of the religions of India as an imperative duty;

And whereas it is necessary to take more effective measure to prevent the commission of sati and its glorification;

Be it enacted by Parliament in the Thirty-eighth Year of Republic of India as follows:

PART I: PRELIMINARY

1. Short Title, Extent and Commencement

(1) This Act may be called the Commission of Sati (Prevention) Act, 1987.

It extends to the whole of India except the State of Jammu and Kashmir.

(3) It shall come into force in a State on such date as the Central Government may, by notification in the Official Gazette, appoint, and different dates may be appointed for different States.

2. Definitions

(1) In this Act, unless the context otherwise requires.-

(a) "Code" means the Code of Criminal Procedure, 1973 (2 of 1974);

(b) "glorification" in relation to *sati,* whether such *sati*, was committed before or after the commencement of this Act, includes, among other things.-

(i) the observance of any ceremony or the taking out of a procession in connection with the commission of *sati*; or

(ii) the supporting, justifying or propagating the practice of *sati* in any manner; or

(iii) the arranging of any function to eulogise the person who has committed sati; or

(iv) the creation of a trust, or the collection of funds, or the construction of temple or other structure or the carrying on of any form of worship or the performance of any ceremony thereat, with a view to perpetuate the honour of, or to preserve the memory of, a person who has committed sati;

(c) "*sati*" means the burning or burying alive of –

(i) any widow along with the body of her deceased husband or any other relative or with any article, object or thing associated with the husband or such relative; or

(ii) any woman along with the body of any of her relatives, irrespective of whether such burning or burying is claimed to be voluntary on the part of the widow or the women or other-wise;

"Special Court" means a Special Court constituted under Sec.9;

(e) "temple" includes any building or other structure, whether roofed or not, constructed or made to preserve the memory or a person in respect of whom sati has been committed or used or intended to be used for the carrying on of any form of worship or for the observance of any ceremony in connection with such commission.

(2) Words and expressions used but not defined in this Act and defined in the Indian Penal Code (45 of 1860) or in the Code shall have the same meanings as are respectively assigned to them in the Indian Panel Code or the Code.

PART II: PUNISHMENT FOR OFFENCES RELATING TO SATI

3. Attempt to Commit Sati

Notwithstanding anything contained in the Indian Penal Code (45 of 1860), whoever attempts to commit sati and does any act towards such commission shall be punishable with imprisonment for a term which may extend to one year or with fine or with both:

Provided that the Special Court trying an offence under this section shall, before convicting any person, take into consideration the circumstances leading to the commission of the offence, the act committed, the state of mind of the person charge of the offence at the time of the commission of the act and all other relevant factors.

4. Abetment of Sati

(1) Notwithstanding anything contained in the Indian Penal Code (45 of 1860), if any person commits *sati*, whoever abets the commission of such sati, either directly or indirectly, shall be punishable with death or imprisonment for life and shall also be liable to fine.

(2) If any person attempts to commit *sati*, whoever abets such attempt, either directly or indirectly, shall be punishable with imprisonment for life and shall also be liable to fine.

Explanation.- For the purposes of this section, any of the following acts or the like shall also be deemed to be an abetment, namely:

(a) any inducement to a widow or woman to get her burnt or buried alive along with the body of her deceased husband or with any other relative or with any article, object or thing associated with the husband or such relative, irrespective of whether she is in a fit state of mind or is labouring under a state of intoxication or stupefaction or other cause impeding the exercise of her free will;

(b) making a widow or woman believe that the commission of *sati* would result in some spiritual benefit to her or her deceased husband or relative or the general well being of the family;

(c) encouraging a widow or woman to remain fixed in her resolve to commit *sati* and thus instigating her to commit *sati*;

(d) participating in any procession in connection with

the commission of *sati* or aiding the widow or woman in her decision to commit sati by taking her along with the body of her deceased husband or relative to the cremation or burial ground;

(e) being present at the place where *sati* is committed as an active participant to such commission or to any ceremony connected with it;

(f) preventing or obstructing the widow or woman from saving herself from being burnt or buried alive;

(g) obstructing, or interfering with, the police in the discharge of its duties of taking any steps to prevent the commission of *sati*.

5. Punishment for Glorification of Sati

Whoever does any act for the glorification of sati shall be punishable with imprisonment for a term which shall not be less than one year but which may extend to seven years and with fine which shall not be less than five thousand rupees but which may extend to thirty thousand rupees.

PART III: POWERS OF COLLECTOR OR DISTRICT MAGISTRATE TO PREVENT OFFENCES RELATING TO SATI

6. Power to Prohibit Certain Acts

(1) where the Collector or the District Magistrate is of the opinion that *sati* or any abetment thereof is being, or is about to be committed, he may, by order, prohibit the doing of any act towards the commission of *sati* by any person in any area or areas specified in the order.

(2) The Collector or the District Magistrate may also, by order, prohibit the glorification in any manner of *sati* by any person in any area or areas specified in the order.

(3) Whoever contravenes any order made under sub-section (1) or sub-section (2) shall, if such contravention is not punishable under any other provision of this Act, be punishable with imprisonment for a term which shali not be less than one year but which may extend to seven years and with fine which shall not be less than five thousand rupees but which may extend to thirty thousand rupees.

7. Power to Remove Certain Temples or Other Structures

(1) The State Government may, if it is satisfied that in that any temple or other structure which has been in existence for not less than twenty years, any form of worship or the performance of any ceremony is carried on with a view to perpetuate the honour of or to preserve the memory of, any person in respect of whom *sati* has been committed, by order, direct the removal of such temple or other structure.

(2) The Collector or the District magistrate may, if he is satisfied that in any temple or other structure, other than that referred to in sub-section (1), any form of worship or the performance of any ceremony is carried on with a view to perpetuate the honour of, or to preserve the memory of, any person in respect of whom *sati* has been committed, by order, direct the removal of such temple or other structure.

(3) Where any order under sub-section (1) or sub-section (2) is not complied with, the State Government or the Collector or the District Magistrate, as the case may be, shall cause the temple or other structure to be removed through a police officer not below the rank of a Sub-Inspector at the cost of the defaulter.

8. Power to Seize Certain Properties

(1) Where the Collector or the District Magistrate has reason to believe that any funds or property have been

collected or acquired for the purpose of glorification of the commission of any *sati* or which may be found under circumstances which create suspicion of the commission of any offence under this Act, he may seize such funds or property.

(2) Every Collector or District Magistrate acting under sub-section (1) shall report the seizure to the Special Court, if any, constituted to try any offence in relation to which such funds or property were collected or acquired and shall await the orders of such Special Court as to the disposal of the same.

PART IV: SPECIAL COURTS

9. Trial of Offences Under this Act

(1) Notwithstanding anything contained in the Code, all offences under this Act shall be triable only by a Special Court constituted under this section.

(2) The State Government shall, by notification in the official Gazette, constitute one or more Special Courts for the trial of offences under this Act and every Special Court shall exercise jurisdiction in respect of the whole or such part of the State as may be specified in the notification.

(3) A Special Court shall be presided over by a judge to be appointed by the State Government with the concurrence of the Chief Justice of the High Court.

(4) A person shall not be qualified for appointment as a judge of a Special Court unless he is, immediately before such appointment, a Sessions Judge or an Additional Sessions Judge in any State.

10. Special Public Prosecutions

(1) For every Special Court, the State Government shall appoint a person to be a Special Public Prosecutor.

(2) A person shall be eligible to be appointed as a Special Public Prosecutor under this section only if he had been in practice as an advocate for not less than seven years or has held any post for a period of not less than seven years under the State requiring special knowledge of law.

(3) Every person appointed as a Special Public Prosecutor under this section shall be deemed to be a Public Prosecutor within the meaning of Cl. (u) of Sec. 2 of the Code and the Provisions of the Code shall have effect accordingly.

11. Procedure and Powers of Special Courts

(1) A Special Court may take cognizance of any offence, without the accused being committed to it for trial, upon receiving a complaint of facts which constitute such offence, or upon a police report of such facts.

(2) Subject to the other provisions of this Act, a Special Court shall for the purpose of the trial of any offence, have all the powers of a Court of Session and shall try such offence as if it were a Court of Session, so far as may be, in accordance with the procedure prescribed in the Code for trial before a Court of Session.

12. Power of Special Court with Respect to Other Offences

(1) When trying any offence under this Act, a Special Court may also try any other offence with which the accused may, under the Code, be charged at the same trial if the offence is connected with such other offence.

(2) If, in the course of any trial of any offence under this Act it is found that the accused person has committed any other offence under this Act or any other law, a Special Court may convict such person also of such other offence

and pass any sentence authorised by this Act or such other law for the punishment thereof.

(3) In every inquiry or trial, the proceedings shall be held as expeditiously as possible and, in particular, where the examination of witnesses has begun, the same shall be continued from day to day until all the witnesses in attendance have been examined, and if any Special Court finds the adjournment of the same beyond the following date to be necessary, it shall record its reasons for doing so.

13. Forfeiture of Funds or Property

Where a person has been convicted of an offence under this Act, the Special Court trying such offence may, if it is considered necessary so to do, declare that any funds or property seized under Sec. 8 shall stand forfeited to the State.

14. Appeal

Notwithstanding anything contained in the Code, an appeal shall lie as a matter of right from any judgement, sentence or order, not being an interlocutory order, of a Special Court to the High Court both of facts and on law.

(2) Every appeal under this section shall be preferred within a period of thirty days from the date of judgment, sentence or order appealed from:

> Provided that the High Court may entertain an appeal after the expiry of the said period of thirty days if it is satisfied that the appellant had sufficient cause for not preferring the appeal within the period of thirty days.

PART V: MISCELLANEOUS

15. Protection of Action Taken Under this Act

No suit, prosecution or other legal proceeding shall lie

against the State Government or any officer or authority of the State Government for anything which is in good faith done or intended to be done in pursuance of this Act or any rules or orders made under this Act.

16. Burden of Proof

Where any person is prosecuted of an offence under Sec. 4, the burden of proving that he had not committed the offence under the said section shall be on him.

17. Obligation of Certain Persons to Report about the Commission of Offence Under this Act

(1) All officers of Government are hereby required and empowered to assist the police in the execution of the provisions of this Act or any rule or order made there under.

(2) All village officers and such other officers as may be specified by the Collector or the District Magistrate in relation to any area and the inhabitants of such area shall, if they have reason to believe or have the knowledge that *sati* is about to be, or has been, committed in the area shall forthwith report such fact to the nearest police station.

(3) Whoever contravenes the provision of sub-section (1) or sub-section (2) shall be punishable with imprisonment of either description for a term which may extend to two years and shall also be liable to fine.

18. Person Convicted of an Offence Under Sec. 4 to be Disqualified form Inheriting Certain Properties

A person convicted of an offence under sub-section (1) of Sec. 4 in relation to the commission of *sati* shall be disqualified from inheriting the property of the person in respect of whom such *sati* has been committed or the property of any other person which he would have been entitled to inherit on the death of person in respect of whom such *sati* has been committed.

Amendment of Act 43 of 1951

In the Representation of the People Act, 1951.-

(a) in Sec. 8, in sub-section (2) after the proviso, the following proviso shall be inserted, namely;

"Provided further that a person convicted by a Special Court for the contravention of any of the provisions of the Commission of Sati (Prevention) Act, 1987 shall be disqualified from the date of such conviction and shall continue to be disqualified for a further period of five years since his release";

(b) in Sec. 123 after Cl.(3-A), the following clause shall be inserted, namely:

"(3-B) The propagation of the practice or the commission of sati or its glorification by a candidate or his agent or any other person with the consent of the candidate or his election agent for the furtherance of the prospects of the election of that candidate or for prejudicially affecting the election of any candidate.

Explanation.- For the purpose of this clause, "*sati*" and "glorification" in relation to *sati* shall have the meanings respectively assigned to them in the Commission of Sati (Prevention) Act, 1987."

20. Act to have Pverriding Effect

The provision of this Act or any rule or order made thereunder shall have effect notwithstanding anything inconsistent therewith contained in any enactment other than this Act or in any instrument having effect by virtue of any enactment other than this Act.

21. Power to Make Rules

(1) The Central Government may, by notification in the Official Gazette, make rules for carrying out the provisions of this Act.

(2) Every rule made under this section shall be laid, as soon as may be after it is made, before each House of Parliament, while it is in session, for a total period of thirty days which may be comprised in one session or in two or more successive sessions, and if, before the expiry of the session immediately following the session or the successive sessions aforesaid, both Houses agree in making any modification in the rule or both Houses agree that the rule should not be made, the rule shall thereafter have effect only in such modified form or be of no effect, as the case may be; so however, that any such modification or annulment shall be without prejudice to the validity of anything previously done under that rule.

Repeal of Existing Laws

(1) All laws in force in any State immediately before the commencement of this Act in that State which provide for the prevention or the glorification of *sati* shall, on such comment, stand repealed.

(2) Notwithstanding, such repeal, anything done or any action taken under any law repealed under sub-section (1) shall be deemed to have been done or taken under the corresponding provisions of this Act, and, in particular, any case taken cognizance of by a Special Court under the provisions of any law so repealed and pending before it immediately before the commencement of this Act in that State shall continue to be dealt with by that Special Court after such commencement as if such Special Court had been constituted under Sec. 9 of this Act.

COMMISSION OF SATI (PREVENTION) RULES, 1988

G.S.R. 360(E), dated 21st March, 1988.- In exercise of the powers conferred by Sec. 21 of the Commission of Sati (Prevention) Act, 1987 (3 of 1988), the Central Government hereby makes the following rules, namely:

1. Short Title and Commencement

(1) These rules may be called the Commission of Sati (Prevention) Rules, 1988.

(2) They shall come into force on the date of their publication in the Official Gazette.

2. Definitions

(1) In these rules, unless the context otherwise requires,-

"Act" means the Commission of Sati (Prevention) Act, 1987 (3 of 1988);

"prohibitory order" means an order issued under Sec. 6;

"section" means section of the Act.

(2) Words and expressions used but not defined in these rules and defined in the Act shall have the same meanings as are respectively assigned to them in the Act.

3. Delegation of Power to Prohibit Certain Acts

(1) The State Government may, by order and subject to such conditions as it may deem fit to impose, direct that the powers of the Collector or the District Magistrate under Sec. 6 may also be exercised by such other officers not below the rank of the village officers.

4. Prohibitory Orders Under Sec. 6, How Made

(1) Every prohibitory order under Sec. 6 shall be made

by beat of drum or other customary mode, in the concerned village, or in case of town or city, in the locality in which the act prohibited is likely to occur or has taken place.

(2) The prohibitory order shall be displayed at some conspicuous place in the area or areas to which such acts relates and a copy thereof shall also be displayed in the office of the officer issuing the prohibitory order and such display shall be taken as a sufficient notice to all persons concerned in the area of areas to which such order relates.

5. Manner of Making Order for Removal of Temples or Structures Under Sub-section (1) of Sec. 7

(1) Before making any order under sub-section (1) of Sec. 7 for removal of any temple or structure, the State Government or any other officer authorized by the State Government in this behalf, shall give at least ninety days' notice to the person or persons involved in the acts complained of, and also to the owners and occupiers of the temple or structure proposed to be removed.

(2) The notice under sub-rule (1) shall specify-

(1) the temple/structure proposed to be removed, its location and other particulars,

(2) the owners/occupiers of the temple/structure, and

(3) the specific instance or instances or worship or ceremony contravening the provisions of Sec.7.

(3) The Government or the officer authorized by the State Government in this behalf shall, after giving reasonable opportunity of being heard to the persons specified in the notice, order the removal of the temple or structure through a police not below the rank of the Sub-Inspector.

6. Manner of Making Order for Removal of Temples or Structures Under Sub-section (2) of Sec. 7

(1) After issue of a prohibitory order under Sec. 6, the Collector or the District Magistrate, or such other officer as directed by the State Government by order under rule 3 shall, before making any order for removal of any temple or structure under sub-section (2) of Sec. 7 give at least ninety days' notice to the owners and occupiers of the temple or structure proposed to be removed.

(2) The Collector of the District Magistrate, or such other officer as directed by the State Government by order under rule3, shall follow the provisions of sub-rules (2) and (3) of rule 4 in the case of orders made under this rule.

7. Inventory and Forfeiture of the Property of Temple or Structure

As soon as the order of removal of the temple or structure is executed, the State Government or the Collector or the District Magistrate, or as the case may be, the officer as directed by the State Government by order under rule 3, shall prepare an inventory of all the material and other property obtained after removal of such temple or structure specifying in it the place where it is lodged or kept, and shall forward the intimation thereof to the Special court for declaration of forfeiture of the said material or property to the State under Sec. 13, if the Special Court considers it necessary so to do, and shall also give a copy of the inventory to the owners/occupiers of the temple/structure removed.

10

The Muslim Women (Protection of Rights on Divorce) Act (1986)

(25 of 1986)(19th May, 1986)

An Act to protect the rights of Muslim women who have been divorced by, or have obtained divorce from, their husbands and to provide for matters connected therewith or incidental thereto.

Be it enacted by Parliament in the Thirty-seventh year of the Republic of India as follows :

1. Short Title and Extent

(1) This Act may be called The Muslim Women (Protection of Rights on Divorce) Act, 1986.

(2) It extends to the whole of India except the State of Jammu and Kashmir.

2. Definitions

In this Act, unless context otherwise requires :

(a) "divorced woman" means a Muslim woman who was married according to Muslim law, and has been divorced by, or has obtained divorce from, her husband in accordance with Muslim law :

(b) "iddat period" means, in the case of a divorced woman, -

(i) three menstrual courses after the date of divorce, if she is subject to menstruation ;

(ii) three lunar months after her divorce, if she is not subject to menstruation ; and

(iii) if she is enceinte at the time of her divorce, the period between the divorce and the delivery of her child or the termination of her pregnancy, whichever is earlier.

(c) "Magistrate" means a Magistrate of the First class exercising jurisdiction under the Code of Criminal Procedure, 1973 (2 of 1974) in the area where the divorced woman resides ;

(d) "prescribed" means prescribed by rules made under the Act.

3. Mahr or Other Properties of Muslim Woman to be Given to Her at the Time of Divorce

(1) Notwithstanding anything contained in any other law for the time being in force, a divorced woman shall be entitled to -

(a) a reasonable and fair provision and maintenance to be made and paid to her within the iddat period by her former husband ;

(b) where she herself maintains the children born to her before or after her divorce, a reasonable and fair provision and maintenance to be made and paid by her former husband for a period of two years from the respective dates of birth of such children ;

(c) an amount equal to the sum of mahr or dower

agreed to be paid to her at the time of her marriage or at any time thereafter according to Muslim law ; and

(d) all the properties given to her before or at the time of marriage or after her marriage by her relatives or friends or the husband or any relatives of the husband or his friends.

(2) Where a reasonable and fair provision and maintenance or the amount of mahr or dower due has not been made or paid or the properties referred to in clause (d) of sub-section (1) have not been delivered to a divorced woman or her divorce, she or any one duly authorised by her may, on her behalf, make an application to the Magistrate for an order for payment of such provision and maintenance, mahr or dower or the delivery of properties, as the case may be.

(3) Where an application has been made under sub-section (2) by a divorced woman, the Magistrate may, if he is satisfied that -

(a) her husband having sufficient means, has failed or neglected to make or pay her within the iddat period a reasonable and fair provision and maintenance for her and the children ; or

(b) the amount equal to the sum of mahr or dower has not been paid or that the properties referred to in clause (d) of sub-section (1) have not been delivered to her, make an order, within one month of the date of filing of the application, directing her former husband to pay such reasonable and fair provision and maintenance to the divorced woman as he may determine as fit and proper having regard to the needs of the divorced woman, the standard of life enjoyed by her during her marriage and the means of her former husband or, as the case may be for the payment of such mahr or dower or the delivery of such properties referred to in clause (d) of sub-section (1) to the divorced woman :

Provided that if the Magistrate finds it impracticable to dispose of the application within the said period, he may, for reasons to be recorded by him, dispose of the application after the said period.

(4) If any person against whom an order has been made under sub-section (3) fails without sufficient cause to comply with the order, the Magistrate may issue a warrant for levying the amount of maintenance or mahr or dower due in the manner provided for levying fines under the Code of Criminal Procedure, 1973 (2 of 1974), and may sentence such person, for the whole or part of any amount remaining unpaid after the execution of the warrant, to imprisonment for a term which may extend to one year or until payment if sooner made, subject to such person being heard in defence and the said sentence being imposed according to the provisions of the said Code.

4. Order for Payment of Maintenance

(1) Notwithstanding anything contained in the foregoing provisions of this Act or in any other law for the time being in force, where a Magistrate is satisfied that a divorced woman has not re-married and is not able to maintain herself after the iddat period, he may make an order directing such of her relatives as would be entitled to inherit her property on her death according to Muslim law to pay such reasonable and fair maintenance

to her as he may determine fit and proper, having regard to the needs of the divorced woman, the standard of life enjoyed by her during her marriage and the means of such relatives and such maintenance shall be payable by such relatives in the proportions in which they would inherit her property and at such period as he may specify in his order :

> Provided that where such divorced woman has children, the Magistrate shall order only such children to pay maintenance to her, and in the event of any such children being unable to pay such maintenance, the Magistrate shall order the parents of such divorced woman to pay maintenance to her :
>
> Provided further that if any of the parents is unable to pay his or her share of the maintenance ordered by the Magistrate on the ground of his or her not having the means to pay the same, the Magistrate may, on proof of such inability being furnished to him, order that the share of such relatives in the maintenance ordered by him be paid by such of the other relatives as may appear to the magistrate to have the means of paying the same in such proportions as the Magistrate may think fit to order :

(2) Where a divorced woman is unable to maintain herself and she has no relatives, as mentioned in sub-section (1) or such relatives or any one of them have not enough means to pay the maintenance ordered by the Magistrate or the other relatives, have not the means to pay the share of those relatives whose shares have been ordered by the Magistrate to be paid by such, other relatives under the second proviso to sub-section (1), the Magistrate may, by order, direct the State Wakf Board established under section 9 of the Wakf Act, 1954 (29 of 1954) or under any other law for the time being in force in a State, functioning in the area in which the

woman resides, to pay such maintenance as, determined by him under sub-section (1) or, as the case may be, to pay the shares of such of the relatives who are unable to pay, at such periods as he may specify in his order.

5. Option to be Governed by the Provisions of Section 125 to 128 of Act (2 of 1974)

If on the date of the first hearing of the application under sub-section (2) of section 3, a divorced woman and her former husband declare, by affidavit or any other declaration in writing in such form as may be prescribed, either jointly or separately, that they would prefer to be governed by the provisions of sections 125 to 128 of the Code of Criminal Procedure, 1973 (2 of 1974), and file such affidavit or declaration in the court hearing the application, the Magistrate shall dispose of such application accordingly.

Explanation - For the purposes of this section, "date of the first hearing of the application" means the date fixed in the summons for the attendance of the respondent to the application.

6. Power to Make Rules

(1) The Central Government may, by notification in the Official Gazette, make rules for carrying out the purposes of this Act.

(2) In particular and without prejudice to the foregoing power such rules may provide for -

(a) the form of the affidavit or other declaration in writing to be filed under section 5 ;

(b) the procedure to be followed by the Magistrate in disposing of applications under this Act, including the serving of notices to the parties to such applications, dates of hearing of such applications and other matters ;

(c) any other matter which is required to be or may be prescribed.

(3) Every rule made under the Act shall be laid, as soon as may be after it is made, before each House of Parliament, while it is in session, for a total period of thirty days which may be comprised in one session or in two or more successive sessions, and if, before the expiry of the session immediately following the session or the modification in the rule or both Houses agree that the rule should not be made, the rule shall thereafter have effect only in such modified form or be of no effect, as the case may be; so, however, that any such modification or annulment shall be without prejudice to the validity of anything previously done under that rule.

7. Transitional Provisions

Every application by a divorced woman under section 125 or under section 127 of the Code of Criminal Procedure, 1973 (2 of 1984) pending before a Magistrate on the commencement of this Act, shall, notwithstanding anything contained in that Code and subject to the provisions of section 5 of this Act, be disposed of by such Magistrate in accordance with the provisions of this Act.

11

Protocol Against the Smuggling of Migrants by Land, Sea and Air, Supplementing the United Nations Convention Against Transnational Crime (2004)

G.A. Res. 55/25, annex III, U.N. GAOR, 55th Sess., Supp. No. 49, at 65, U.N. Doc. A/45/49 (Vol. I) (2001), Entered into force Jan. 28, 2004

Preamble

The States Parties to this Protocol,

Declaring that effective action to prevent and combat the smuggling of migrants by land, sea and air requires a comprehensive international approach, including cooperation, the exchange of information and other appropriate measures, including socio-economic measures, at the national, regional and international levels,

Recalling General Assembly resolution 54/212 of 22 December 1999, in which the Assembly urged Member States and the United Nations system to strengthen international cooperation in the area of international migration and development in order to address the root causes of migration, especially those related to poverty, and to maximize the benefits of international migration to those concerned, and encouraged, where relevant, interregional, regional and subregional mechanisms to continue to address the question of migration and development,

Convinced of the need to provide migrants with humane treatment and full protection of their rights,

Taking into account the fact that, despite work undertaken in other international forums, there is no universal instrument that addresses all aspects of smuggling of migrants and other related issues,

Concerned at the significant increase in the activities of organized criminal groups in smuggling of migrants and other related criminal activities set forth in this Protocol, which bring great harm to the States concerned,

Also concerned that the smuggling of migrants can endanger the lives or security of the migrants involved,

Recalling General Assembly resolution 53/111 of 9 December 1998, in which the Assembly decided to establish an open-ended intergovernmental ad hoc committee for the purpose of elaborating a comprehensive international convention against transnational organized crime and of discussing the elaboration of, inter alia, an international instrument addressing illegal trafficking in and transporting of migrants, including by sea,

Convinced that supplementing the United Nations Convention against Transnational Organized Crime with an international instrument against the smuggling of migrants by land, sea and air will be useful in preventing and combating that crime,

Have agreed as follows:

I. GENERAL PROVISIONS

Article 1

Relation with the United Nations Convention against Transnational Organized Crime

1. This Protocol supplements the United Nations Convention against Transnational Organized Crime. It shall be interpreted together with the Convention.

2. The provisions of the Convention shall apply, mutatis mutandis, to this Protocol unless otherwise provided herein.

3. The offences established in accordance with article 6 of this Protocol shall be regarded as offences established in accordance with the Convention.

Article 2

Statement of purpose

The purpose of this Protocol is to prevent and combat the smuggling of migrants, as well as to promote cooperation among States Parties to that end, while protecting the rights of smuggled migrants.

Article 3

Use of terms

For the purposes of this Protocol:

(a) "Smuggling of migrants" shall mean the procurement, in order to obtain, directly or indirectly, a financial or other material benefit, of the illegal entry of a person into a State Party of which the person is not a national or a permanent resident;

(b) "Illegal entry" shall mean crossing borders without complying with the necessary requirements for legal entry into the receiving State;

(c) "Fraudulent travel or identity document" shall mean any travel or identity document:

  (i) That has been falsely made or altered in some material way by anyone other than a person or agency lawfully authorized to make or issue the travel or identity document on behalf of a State; or

  (ii) That has been improperly issued or obtained through misrepresentation, corruption or duress or in any other unlawful manner; or

(iii) That is being used by a person other than the rightful holder;

(d) "Vessel" shall mean any type of water craft, including non-displacement craft and seaplanes, used or capable of being used as a means of transportation on water, except a warship, naval auxiliary or other vessel owned or operated by a Government and used, for the time being, only on government non-commercial service.

Article 4

Scope of application

This Protocol shall apply, except as otherwise stated herein, to the prevention, investigation and prosecution of the offences established in accordance with article 6 of this Protocol, where the offences are transnational in nature and involve an organized criminal group, as well as to the protection of the rights of persons who have been the object of such offences.

Article 5

Criminal liability of migrants

Migrants shall not become liable to criminal prosecution

under this Protocol for the fact of having been the object of conduct set forth in article 6 of this Protocol.

Article 6

Criminalization

1. Each State Party shall adopt such legislative and other measures as may be necessary to establish as criminal offences, when committed intentionally and in order to obtain, directly or indirectly, a financial or other material benefit:

(a) The smuggling of migrants;

(b) When committed for the purpose of enabling the smuggling of migrants:

(i) Producing a fraudulent travel or identity document;

(ii) Procuring, providing or possessing such a document;

(c) Enabling a person who is not a national or a permanent resident to remain in the State concerned without complying with the necessary requirements for legally remaining in the State by the means mentioned in subparagraph (b) of this paragraph or any other illegal means.

2. Each State Party shall also adopt such legislative and other measures as may be necessary to establish as criminal offences:

(a) Subject to the basic concepts of its legal system, attempting to commit an offence established in accordance with paragraph 1 of this article;

(b) Participating as an accomplice in an offence established in accordance with paragraph 1 (a), (b)

(i) or (c) of this article and, subject to the basic concepts of its legal system, participating as an accomplice in an offence established in accordance with paragraph 1 (b) (ii) of this article;

(c) Organizing or directing other persons to commit an offence established in accordance with paragraph 1 of this article.

3. Each State Party shall adopt such legislative and other measures as may be necessary to establish as aggravating circumstances to the offences established in accordance with paragraph 1 (a), (b) (i) and (c) of this article and, subject to the basic concepts of its legal system, to the offences established in accordance with paragraph 2 (b) and (c) of this article, circumstances:

(a) That endanger, or are likely to endanger, the lives or safety of the migrants concerned; or

(b) That entail inhuman or degrading treatment, including for exploitation, of such migrants.

4. Nothing in this Protocol shall prevent a State Party from taking measures against a person whose conduct constitutes an offence under its domestic law.

II. SMUGGLING OF MIGRANTS BY SEA

Article 7

Cooperation

States Parties shall cooperate to the fullest extent possible to prevent and suppress the smuggling of migrants by sea, in accordance with the international law of the sea.

Article 8

Measures against the smuggling of migrants by sea

1. A State Party that has reasonable grounds to suspect that a vessel that is flying its flag or claiming its registry, that is without nationality or that, though flying a foreign flag or refusing to show a flag, is in reality of the nationality of the State Party concerned is engaged in the smuggling of migrants by sea may request the assistance of other States Parties in suppressing the use of the vessel for that purpose. The States Parties so requested shall render such assistance to the extent possible within their means.

2. A State Party that has reasonable grounds to suspect that a vessel exercising freedom of navigation in accordance with international law and flying the flag or displaying the marks of registry of another State Party is engaged in the smuggling of migrants by sea may so notify the flag State, request confirmation of registry and, if confirmed, request authorization from the flag State to take appropriate measures with regard to that vessel. The flag State may authorize the requesting State, inter alia:

(a) To board the vessel;

(b) To search the vessel; and

(c) If evidence is found that the vessel is engaged in the smuggling of migrants by sea, to take appropriate measures with respect to the vessel and persons and cargo on board, as authorized by the flag State.

3. A State Party that has taken any measure in accordance with paragraph 2 of this article shall promptly inform the flag State concerned of the results of that measure.

4. A State Party shall respond expeditiously to a request from another State Party to determine whether a vessel that is claiming its registry or flying its flag is entitled to do so and to a request for authorization made in accordance with paragraph 2 of this article.

5. A flag State may, consistent with article 7 of this Protocol, subject its authorization to conditions to be agreed by it and the requesting State, including conditions relating to responsibility and the extent of effective measures to be taken. A State Party shall take no additional measures without the express authorization of the flag State, except those necessary to relieve imminent danger to the lives of persons or those which derive from relevant bilateral or multilateral agreements.

6. Each State Party shall designate an authority or, where necessary, authorities to receive and respond to requests for assistance, for confirmation of registry or of the right of a vessel to fly its flag and for authorization to take appropriate measures. Such designation shall be notified through the Secretary-General to all other States Parties within one month of the designation.

7. A State Party that has reasonable grounds to suspect that a vessel is engaged in the smuggling of migrants by sea and is without nationality or may be assimilated to a vessel without nationality may board and search the vessel. If evidence confirming the suspicion is found, that State Party shall take appropriate measures in accordance with relevant domestic and international law.

Article 9

Safeguard clauses

1. Where a State Party takes measures against a vessel in accordance with article 8 of this Protocol, it shall:

(a) Ensure the safety and humane treatment of the persons on board;

(b) Take due account of the need not to endanger the security of the vessel or its cargo;

(c) Take due account of the need not to prejudice the commercial or legal interests of the flag State or any other interested State;

(d) Ensure, within available means, that any measure taken with regard to the vessel is environmentally sound.

2. Where the grounds for measures taken pursuant to article 8 of this Protocol prove to be unfounded, the vessel shall be compensated for any loss or damage that may have been sustained, provided that the vessel has not committed any act justifying the measures taken.

3. Any measure taken, adopted or implemented in accordance with this chapter shall take due account of the need not to interfere with or to affect:

(a) The rights and obligations and the exercise of jurisdiction of coastal States in accordance with the international law of the sea; or

(b) The authority of the flag State to exercise jurisdiction and control in administrative, technical and social matters involving the vessel.

4. Any measure taken at sea pursuant to this chapter shall be carried out only by warships or military aircraft, or by other ships or aircraft clearly marked and identifiable as being on government service and authorized to that effect.

III. PREVENTION, COOPERATION AND OTHER MEASURES

Article 10

Information

1. Without prejudice to articles 27 and 28 of the

Convention, States Parties, in particular those with common borders or located on routes along which migrants are smuggled, shall, for the purpose of achieving the objectives of this Protocol, exchange among themselves, consistent with their respective domestic legal and administrative systems, relevant information on matters such as:

(a) Embarkation and destination points, as well as routes, carriers and means of transportation, known to be or suspected of being used by an organized criminal group engaged in conduct set forth in article 6 of this Protocol;

(b) The identity and methods of organizations or organized criminal groups known to be or suspected of being engaged in conduct set forth in article 6 of this Protocol;

(c) The authenticity and proper form of travel documents issued by a State Party and the theft or related misuse of blank travel or identity documents;

(d) Means and methods of concealment and transportation of persons, the unlawful alteration, reproduction or acquisition or other misuse of travel or identity documents used in conduct set forth in article 6 of this Protocol and ways of detecting them;

(e) Legislative experiences and practices and measures to prevent and combat the conduct set forth in article 6 of this Protocol; and

(f) Scientific and technological information useful to law enforcement, so as to enhance each other's ability to prevent, detect and investigate the conduct set forth in article 6 of this Protocol and to prosecute those involved.

2. A State Party that receives information shall comply with any request by the State Party that transmitted the information that places restrictions on its use.

Article 11

Border measures

1. Without prejudice to international commitments in relation to the free movement of people, States Parties shall strengthen, to the extent possible, such border controls as may be necessary to prevent and detect the smuggling of migrants.

2. Each State Party shall adopt legislative or other appropriate measures to prevent, to the extent possible, means of transport operated by commercial carriers from being used in the commission of the offence established in accordance with article 6, paragraph 1 (a), of this Protocol.

3. Where appropriate, and without prejudice to applicable international conventions, such measures shall include establishing the obligation of commercial carriers, including any transportation company or the owner or operator of any means of transport, to ascertain that all passengers are in possession of the travel documents required for entry into the receiving State.

4. Each State Party shall take the necessary measures, in accordance with its domestic law, to provide for sanctions in cases of violation of the obligation set forth in paragraph 3 of this article.

5. Each State Party shall consider taking measures that permit, in accordance with its domestic law, the denial of entry or revocation of visas of persons implicated in the commission of offences established in accordance with this Protocol.

6. Without prejudice to article 27 of the Convention, States Parties shall consider strengthening cooperation among border control agencies by, inter alia, establishing and maintaining direct channels of communication.

Article 12

Security and control of documents

Each State Party shall take such measures as may be necessary, within available means:

(a) To ensure that travel or identity documents issued by it are of such quality that they cannot easily be misused and cannot readily be falsified or unlawfully altered, replicated or issued; and

(b) To ensure the integrity and security of travel or identity documents issued by or on behalf of the State Party and to prevent their unlawful creation, issuance and use.

Article 13

Legitimacy and validity of documents

At the request of another State Party, a State Party shall, in accordance with its domestic law, verify within a reasonable time the legitimacy and validity of travel or identity documents issued or purported to have been issued in its name and suspected of being used for purposes of conduct set forth in article 6 of this Protocol.

Article 14

Training and technical cooperation

1. States Parties shall provide or strengthen specialized training for immigration and other relevant officials in preventing the conduct set forth in article 6 of this Protocol and in the humane treatment of migrants who have been

the object of such conduct, while respecting their rights as set forth in this Protocol.

2. States Parties shall cooperate with each other and with competent international organizations, non-governmental organizations, other relevant organizations and other elements of civil society as appropriate to ensure that there is adequate personnel training in their territories to prevent, combat and eradicate the conduct set forth in article 6 of this Protocol and to protect the rights of migrants who have been the object of such conduct. Such training shall include:

(a) Improving the security and quality of travel documents;

(b) Recognizing and detecting fraudulent travel or identity documents;

(c) Gathering criminal intelligence, relating in particular to the identification of organized criminal groups known to be or suspected of being engaged in conduct set forth in article 6 of this Protocol, the methods used to transport smuggled migrants, the misuse of travel or identity documents for purposes of conduct set forth in article 6 and the means of concealment used in the smuggling of migrants;

(d) Improving procedures for detecting smuggled persons at conventional and non-conventional points of entry and exit; and

(e) The humane treatment of migrants and the protection of their rights as set forth in this Protocol.

3. States Parties with relevant expertise shall consider providing technical assistance to States that are frequently countries of origin or transit for persons who have been

the object of conduct set forth in article 6 of this Protocol. States Parties shall make every effort to provide the necessary resources, such as vehicles, computer systems and document readers, to combat the conduct set forth in article 6.

Article 15

Other prevention measures

1. Each State Party shall take measures to ensure that it provides or strengthens information programmes to increase public awareness of the fact that the conduct set forth in article 6 of this Protocol is a criminal activity frequently perpetrated by organized criminal groups for profit and that it poses serious risks to the migrants concerned.

2. In accordance with article 31 of the Convention, States Parties shall cooperate in the field of public information for the purpose of preventing potential migrants from falling victim to organized criminal groups.

3. Each State Party shall promote or strengthen, as appropriate, development programmes and cooperation at the national, regional and international levels, taking into account the socio-economic realities of migration and paying special attention to economically and socially depressed areas, in order to combat the root socio-economic causes of the smuggling of migrants, such as poverty and underdevelopment.

Article 16

Protection and assistance measures

1. In implementing this Protocol, each State Party shall take, consistent with its obligations under international law, all appropriate measures, including legislation if

necessary, to preserve and protect the rights of persons who have been the object of conduct set forth in article 6 of this Protocol as accorded under applicable international law, in particular the right to life and the right not to be subjected to torture or other cruel, inhuman or degrading treatment or punishment.

2. Each State Party shall take appropriate measures to afford migrants appropriate protection against violence that may be inflicted upon them, whether by individuals or groups, by reason of being the object of conduct set forth in article 6 of this Protocol.

3. Each State Party shall afford appropriate assistance to migrants whose lives or safety are endangered by reason of being the object of conduct set forth in article 6 of this Protocol.

4. In applying the provisions of this article, States Parties shall take into account the special needs of women and children.

5. In the case of the detention of a person who has been the object of conduct set forth in article 6 of this Protocol, each State Party shall comply with its obligations under the Vienna Convention on Consular Relations, where applicable, including that of informing the person concerned without delay about the provisions concerning notification to and communication with consular officers.

Article 17

Agreements and arrangements

States Parties shall consider the conclusion of bilateral or regional agreements or operational arrangements or understandings aimed at:

(a) Establishing the most appropriate and effective measures to prevent and combat the conduct set forth in article 6 of this Protocol; or

(b) Enhancing the provisions of this Protocol among themselves.

Article 18

Return of smuggled migrants

1. Each State Party agrees to facilitate and accept, without undue or unreasonable delay, the return of a person who has been the object of conduct set forth in article 6 of this Protocol and who is its national or who has the right of permanent residence in its territory at the time of return.

2. Each State Party shall consider the possibility of facilitating and accepting the return of a person who has been the object of conduct set forth in article 6 of this Protocol and who had the right of permanent residence in its territory at the time of entry into the receiving State in accordance with its domestic law.

3. At the request of the receiving State Party, a requested State Party shall, without undue or unreasonable delay, verify whether a person who has been the object of conduct set forth in article 6 of this Protocol is its national or has the right of permanent residence in its territory.

4. In order to facilitate the return of a person who has been the object of conduct set forth in article 6 of this Protocol and is without proper documentation, the State Party of which that person is a national or in which he or she has the right of permanent residence shall agree to issue, at the request of the receiving State Party, such travel documents or other authorization as may be necessary to enable the person to travel to and re-enter its territory.

5. Each State Party involved with the return of a person who has been the object of conduct set forth in article 6 of this Protocol shall take all appropriate measures to carry out the return in an orderly manner and with due regard for the safety and dignity of the person.

6. States Parties may cooperate with relevant international organizations in the implementation of this article.

7. This article shall be without prejudice to any right afforded to persons who have been the object of conduct set forth in article 6 of this Protocol by any domestic law of the receiving State Party.

8. This article shall not affect the obligations entered into under any other applicable treaty, bilateral or multilateral, or any other applicable operational agreement or arrangement that governs, in whole or in part, the return of persons who have been the object of conduct set forth in article 6 of this Protocol.

IV. FINAL PROVISIONS

Article 19

Saving clause

1. Nothing in this Protocol shall affect the other rights, obligations and responsibilities of States and individuals under international law, including international humanitarian law and international human rights law and, in particular, where applicable, the 1951 Convention and the 1967 Protocol relating to the Status of Refugees and the principle of non-refoulement as contained therein.

2. The measures set forth in this Protocol shall be

interpreted and applied in a way that is not discriminatory to persons on the ground that they are the object of conduct set forth in article 6 of this Protocol. The interpretation and application of those measures shall be consistent with internationally recognized principles of non-discrimination.

Article 20

Settlement of disputes

1. States Parties shall endeavour to settle disputes concerning the interpretation or application of this Protocol through negotiation.

2. Any dispute between two or more States Parties concerning the interpretation or application of this Protocol that cannot be settled through negotiation within a reasonable time shall, at the request of one of those States Parties, be submitted to arbitration. If, six months after the date of the request for arbitration, those States Parties are unable to agree on the organization of the arbitration, any one of those States Parties may refer the dispute to the International Court of Justice by request in accordance with the Statute of the Court.

3. Each State Party may, at the time of signature, ratification, acceptance or approval of or accession to this Protocol, declare that it does not consider itself bound by paragraph 2 of this article. The other States Parties shall not be bound by paragraph 2 of this article with respect to any State Party that has made such a reservation.

4. Any State Party that has made a reservation in accordance with paragraph 3 of this article may at any time withdraw that reservation by notification to the Secretary-General of the United Nations.

Article 21

Signature, ratification, acceptance, approval and accession

1. This Protocol shall be open to all States for signature from 12 to 15 December 2000 in Palermo, Italy, and thereafter at United Nations Headquarters in New York until 12 December 2002.

2. This Protocol shall also be open for signature by regional economic integration organizations provided that at least one member State of such organization has signed this Protocol in accordance with paragraph 1 of this article.

3. This Protocol is subject to ratification, acceptance or approval. Instruments of ratification, acceptance or approval shall be deposited with the Secretary-General of the United Nations. A regional economic integration organization may deposit its instrument of ratification, acceptance or approval if at least one of its member States has done likewise. In that instrument of ratification, acceptance or approval, such organization shall declare the extent of its competence with respect to the matters governed by this Protocol. Such organization shall also inform the depositary of any relevant modification in the extent of its competence.

4. This Protocol is open for accession by any State or any regional economic integration organization of which at least one member State is a Party to this Protocol. Instruments of accession shall be deposited with the Secretary-General of the United Nations. At the time of its accession, a regional economic integration organization shall declare the extent of its competence with respect to matters governed by this Protocol. Such organization shall also inform the depositary of any relevant modification in the extent of its competence.

Article 22

Entry into force

1. This Protocol shall enter into force on the ninetieth day after the date of deposit of the fortieth instrument of ratification, acceptance, approval or accession, except that it shall not enter into force before the entry into force of the Convention. For the purpose of this paragraph, any instrument deposited by a regional economic integration organization shall not be counted as additional to those deposited by member States of such organization.

2. For each State or regional economic integration organization ratifying, accepting, approving or acceding to this Protocol after the deposit of the fortieth instrument of such action, this Protocol shall enter into force on the thirtieth day after the date of deposit by such State or organization of the relevant instrument or on the date this Protocol enters into force pursuant to paragraph 1 of this article, whichever is the later.

Article 23

Amendment

1. After the expiry of five years from the entry into force of this Protocol, a State Party to the Protocol may propose an amendment and file it with the Secretary-General of the United Nations, who shall thereupon communicate the proposed amendment to the States Parties and to the Conference of the Parties to the Convention for the purpose of considering and deciding on the proposal. The States Parties to this Protocol meeting at the Conference of the Parties shall make every effort to achieve consensus on each amendment. If all efforts at consensus have been exhausted and no agreement has been reached, the amendment shall, as a last resort, require for its adoption

a two-thirds majority vote of the States Parties to this Protocol present and voting at the meeting of the Conference of the Parties.

2. Regional economic integration organizations, in matters within their competence, shall exercise their right to vote under this article with a number of votes equal to the number of their member States that are Parties to this Protocol. Such organizations shall not exercise their right to vote if their member States exercise theirs and vice versa.

3. An amendment adopted in accordance with paragraph 1 of this article is subject to ratification, acceptance or approval by States Parties.

4. An amendment adopted in accordance with paragraph 1 of this article shall enter into force in respect of a State Party ninety days after the date of the deposit with the Secretary-General of the United Nations of an instrument of ratification, acceptance or approval of such amendment.

5. When an amendment enters into force, it shall be binding on those States Parties which have expressed their consent to be bound by it. Other States Parties shall still be bound by the provisions of this Protocol and any earlier amendments that they have ratified, accepted or approved.

Article 24

Denunciation

1. A State Party may denounce this Protocol by written notification to the Secretary-General of the United Nations. Such denunciation shall become effective one year after the date of receipt of the notification by the Secretary-General.

2. A regional economic integration organization shall cease to be a Party to this Protocol when all of its member States have denounced it.

Article 25

Depositary and languages

1. The Secretary-General of the United Nations is designated depositary of this Protocol.

2. The original of this Protocol, of which the Arabic, Chinese, English, French, Russian and Spanish texts are equally authentic, shall be deposited with the Secretary-General of the United Nations.

In witness whereof, the undersigned plenipotentiaries, being duly authorized thereto by their respective Governments, have signed this Protocol.

12

Inter-American Convention on the Prevention, Punishment and Eradication of Violence Against Women (1995)

33 I.L.M. 1534 (1994), Entered into force March 5, 1995.

Preamble

The States Parties to this Convention,

RECOGNIZING that full respect for human rights has been enshrined in the American Declaration of the Rights and Duties of Man and the Universal Declaration of Human Rights, and reaffirmed in other international and regional instruments;

AFFIRMING that violence against women constitutes a violation of their human rights and fundamental freedoms, and impairs or nullifies the observance, enjoyment and exercise of such rights and freedoms;

CONCERNED that violence against women is an offense against human dignity and a manifestation of the historically unequal power relations between women and men;

RECALLING the Declaration on the Elimination of

Violence against Women, adopted by the Twenty-fifth Assembly of Delegates of the Inter-American Commission of Women, and affirming that violence against women pervades every sector of society regardless of class, race or ethnic group, income, culture, level of education, age or religion and strikes at its very foundations;

CONVINCED that the elimination of violence against women is essential for their individual and social development and their full and equal participation in all walks of life; and

CONVINCED that the adoption of a convention on the prevention, punishment and eradication of all forms of violence against women within the framework of the Organization of American States is a positive contribution to protecting the rights of women and eliminating violence against them,

HAVE AGREED to the following:

CHAPTER I: DEFINITION AND SCOPE OF APPLICATION

Article 1

For the purposes of this Convention, violence against women shall be understood as any act or conduct, based on gender, which causes death or physical, sexual or psychological harm or suffering to women, whether in the public or the private sphere.

Article 2

Violence against women shall be understood to include physical, sexual and psychological violence:

a. that occurs within the family or domestic unit or within any other interpersonal relationship, whether or not the perpetrator shares or has shared the same residence with the woman, including, among others, rape, battery and sexual abuse;

b. that occurs in the community and is perpetrated by any person, including, among others, rape, sexual abuse, torture, trafficking in persons, forced prostitution, kidnapping and sexual harassment in the workplace, as well as in educational institutions, health facilities or any other place; and

c. that is perpetrated or condoned by the state or its agents regardless of where it occurs.

CHAPTER II: RIGHTS PROTECTED

Article 3

Every woman has the right to be free from violence in both the public and private spheres.

Article 4

Every woman has the right to the recognition, enjoyment, exercise and protection of all human rights and freedoms embodied in regional and international human rights instruments. These rights include, among others:

a. The right to have her life respected;

b. The right to have her physical, mental and moral integrity respected;

c. The right to personal liberty and security;

d. The right not to be subjected to torture;

e. The right to have the inherent dignity of her person respected and her family protected;

f. The right to equal protection before the law and of the law;

g. The right to simple and prompt recourse to a competent court for protection against acts that violate her rights;

h. The right to associate freely;

i. The right of freedom to profess her religion and beliefs within the law; and

j. The right to have equal access to the public service of her country and to take part in the conduct of public affairs, including decision-making.

Article 5

Every woman is entitled to the free and full exercise of her civil, political, economic, social and cultural rights, and may rely on the full protection of those rights as embodied in regional and international instruments on human rights. The States Parties recognize that violence against women prevents and nullifies the exercise of these rights.

Article 6

The right of every woman to be free from violence includes, among others:

a. The right of women to be free from all forms of discrimination; and

b. The right of women to be valued and educated free of stereotyped patterns of behaviour and social and cultural practices based on concepts of inferiority or subordination.

CHAPTER III: DUTIES OF THE STATES

Article 7

The States Parties condemn all forms of violence against

women and agree to pursue, by all appropriate means and without delay, policies to prevent, punish and eradicate such violence and undertake to:

a. refrain from engaging in any act or practice of violence against women and to ensure that their authorities, officials, personnel, agents, and institutions act in conformity with this obligation;

b. apply due diligence to prevent, investigate and impose penalties for violence against women;

c. include in their domestic legislation penal, civil, administrative and any other type of provisions that may be needed to prevent, punish and eradicate violence against women and to adopt appropriate administrative measures where necessary;

d. adopt legal measures to require the perpetrator to refrain from harassing, intimidating or threatening the woman or using any method that harms or endangers her life or integrity, or damages her property;

e. take all appropriate measures, including legislative measures, to amend or repeal existing laws and regulations or to modify legal or customary practices which sustain the persistence and tolerance of violence against women;

f. establish fair and effective legal procedures for women who have been subjected to violence which include, among others, protective measures, a timely hearing and effective access to such procedures;

g. establish the necessary legal and administrative mechanisms to ensure that women subjected to violence have effective access to restitution, reparations or other just and effective remedies; and

h. adopt such legislative or other measures as may be necessary to give effect to this Convention.

Article 8

The States Parties agree to undertake progressively specific measures, including programmes:

a. to promote awareness and observance of the right of women to be free from violence, and the right of women to have their human rights respected and protected;

b. to modify social and cultural patterns of conduct of men and women, including the development of formal and informal educational programmes appropriate to every level of the educational process, to counteract prejudices, customs and all other practices which are based on the idea of the inferiority or superiority of either of the sexes or on the stereotyped roles for men and women which legitimize or exacerbate violence against women;

c. to promote the education and training of all those involved in the administration of justice, police and other law enforcement officers as well as other personnel responsible for implementing policies for the prevention, punishment and eradication of violence against women;

d. to provide appropriate specialized services for women who have been subjected to violence, through public and private sector agencies, including shelters, counseling services for ail family members where appropriate, and care and custody of the affected children;

e. to promote and support governmental and private sector education designed to raise the awareness of the public with respect to the problems of and remedies for violence against women;

f. to provide women who are subjected to violence access to effective readjustment and training programmes to enable them to fully participate in public, private and social life;

g. to encourage the communications media to develop appropriate media guidelines in order to contribute to the eradication of violence against women in all its forms, and to enhance respect for the dignity of women;

h. to ensure research and the gathering of statistics and other relevant information relating to the causes, consequences and frequency of violence against women, in order to assess the effectiveness of measures to prevent, punish and eradicate violence against women and to formulate and implement the necessary changes; and

i. to foster international cooperation for the exchange of ideas and experiences and the execution of programmes aimed at protecting women who are subjected to violence.

Article 9

With respect to the adoption of the measures in this Chapter, the States Parties shall take special account of the vulnerability of women to violence by reason of,among others, their race or ethnic background or their status as migrants, refugees or displaced persons. Similar consideration shall be given to women subjected to violence while pregnant or who are disabled, of minor age, elderly, socioeconomically disadvantaged, affected by armed conflict or deprived of their freedom.

CHAPTER IV: INTER-AMERICAN MECHANISMS OF PROTECTION

Article 10

In order to protect the right of every woman to be free from violence, the States Parties shall include in their national reports to the Inter-American Commission of Women information on measures adopted to prevent and prohibit violence against women, and to assist women affected by violence, as well as on any difficulties they observe in applying those measures, and the factors that contribute to violence against women.

Article 11

The States Parties to this Convention and the Inter-American Commission of Women may request of the Inter-American Court of Human Rights advisory opinions on the interpretation of this Convention.

Article 12

Any person or group of persons, or any nongovernmental entity legally recognized in one or more member states of the Organization, may lodge petitions with the Inter-American Commission on Human Rights containing denunciations or complaints of violations of Article 7 of this Convention by a State Party, and the Commission shall consider such claims in accordance with the norms and procedures established by the American Convention on Human Rights and the Statutes and Regulations of the Inter-American Commission on Human Rights for lodging and considering petitions.

CHAPTER V: GENERAL PROVISIONS

Article 13

No part of this Convention shall be understood to restrict or limit the domestic law of any State Party that affords equal or greater protection and guarantees of the rights of women and appropriate safeguards to prevent and eradicate violence against women.

Article 14

No part of this Convention shall be understood to restrict or limit the American Convention on Human Rights or any other international convention on the subject that provides for equal or greater protection in this area.

Article 15

This Convention is open to signature by all the member States of the Organization of American States.

Article 16

This Convention is subject to ratification. The instruments of ratification shall be deposited with the General Secretariat of the Organization of American States.

Article 17

This Convention is open to accession by any other state. Instruments of accession shall be deposited with the General Secretariat of the Organization of American States.

Article 18

Any State may, at the time of approval, signature, ratification, or accession, make reservations to this Convention provided that such reservations are:

a. not incompatible with the object and purpose of the Convention, and

b. not of a general nature and relate to one or more specific provisions.

Article 19

Any State Party may submit to the General Assembly, through the Inter-American Commission of Women, proposals for the amendment of this Convention.

Amendments shall enter into force for the states ratifying them on the date when two-thirds of the States Parties to this Convention have deposited their respective instruments of ratification. With respect to the other States Parties, the amendments shall enter into force on the dates on which they deposit their respective instruments of ratification.

Article 20

If a State Party has two or more territorial units in which the matters dealt with in this Convention are governed by different systems of law, it may, at the time of signature, ratification or accession, declare that this Convention shall extend to all its territorial units or to only one or more of them.

Such a declaration may be amended at any time by subsequent declarations, which shall expressly specify the territorial unit or units to which this Convention applies. Such subsequent declarations shall be transmitted to the General Secretariat of the Organization of American States, and shall enter into force thirty days after the date of their receipt.

Article 21

This Convention shall enter into force on the thirtieth day after the date of deposit of the second instrument of ratification. For each State that ratifies or accedes to the

Convention after the second instrument of ratification is deposited, it shall enter into force thirty days after the date on which that State deposited its instrument of ratification or accession.

Article 22

The Secretary General shall inform all member states of the Organization of American States of the entry into force of this Convention.

Article 23

The Secretary General of the Organization of American States shall present an annual report to the member states of the Organization on the status of this Convention, including the signatures, deposits of instruments of ratification and accession, and declarations, and any reservations that may have been presented by the States Parties, accompanied by a report thereon if needed.

Article 24

This Convention shall remain in force indefinitely, but any of the States Parties may denounce it by depositing an instrument to that effect with the General Secretariat of the Organization of American States. One year after the date of deposit of the instrument of denunciation, this Convention shall cease to be in effect for the denouncing State but shall remain in force for the remaining States Parties.

Article 25

The original instrument of this Convention, the English, French, Portuguese and Spanish texts of which are equally authentic, shall be deposited with the General Secretariat of the Organization of American States, which shall send a certified copy to the Secretariat of the United Nations for registration and publication in accordance with the provisions of Article 102 of the United Nations Charter.

In witness whereof, the undersigned Plenipotentiaries, being duly authorized thereto by their respective governments, have signed this Convention, which shall be called the Inter-American Convention on the Prevention, Punishment and Eradication of Violence against Women Convention of Belém do Pará..

Done in the city of Belem Do Para, Brazil the ninth of June in the year one thousand nine hundred ninety-four.

13

Declaration on the Protection of Women and Children in Emergency and Armed Conflict (1974)

G.A. res. 3318 (XXIX), 29 U.N. GAOR Supp. (No. 31) at 146, U.N. Doc. A/9631 (1974)

The General Assembly,

Having considered the recommendation of the Economic and Social Council contained in its resolution 1861 (LVI) of 16 May 1974,

Expressing its deep concern over the sufferings of women and children belonging to the civilian population who in periods of emergency and armed conflict in the struggle for peace, self-determination, national liberation and independence are too often the victims of inhuman acts and consequently suffer serious harm,

Aware of the suffering of women and children in many areas of the world, especially in those areas subject to suppression, aggression, colonialism, racism, alien domination and foreign subjugation,

Deeply concerned by the fact that, despite general and unequivocal condemnation, colonialism, racism and alien and foreign domination continue to subject many peoples under their yoke, cruelly suppressing the national liberation movements and inflicting heavy losses and incalculable sufferings on the populations under their domination, including women and children,

Deploring the fact that grave attacks are still being made on fundamental freedoms and the dignity of the human person and that colonial and racist foreign domination Powers continue to violate international humanitarian law,

Recalling the relevant provisions contained in the instruments of international humanitarian law relative to the protection of women and children in time of peace and war,

Recalling, among other important documents, its resolutions 2444 (XXIII) of 19 December 1968, 2597 (XXIV) of 16 December 1969 and 2674 (XXV) and 2675 (XXV) of 9 December 1970, on respect for human rights and on basic principles for the protection of civilian populations in armed conflicts, as well as Economic and Social Council resolution 1515 (XLVIII) of 28 May 1970 in which the Council requested the General Assembly to consider the possibility of drafting a declaration on the protection of women and children in emergency or wartime,

Conscious of its responsibility for the destiny of the rising generation and for the destiny of mothers, who play an important role in society, in the family and particularly in the upbringing of children,

Bearing in mind the need to provide special protection of women and children belonging to the civilian population,

Solemnly proclaims this Declaration on the Protection

of Women and Children in Emergency and Armed Conflict and calls for the strict observance of the Declaration by all Member States:

1. Attacks and bombings on the civilian population, inflicting incalculable suffering, especially on women and children, who are the most vulnerable members of the population, shall be prohibited, and such acts shall be condemned.

2. The use of chemical and bacteriological weapons in the course of military operations constitutes one of the most flagrant violations of the Geneva Protocol of 1925, the Geneva Conventions of 1949 and the principles of international humanitarian law and inflicts heavy losses on civilian populations, including defenceless women and children, and shall be severely condemned.

3. All States shall abide fully by their obligations under the Geneva Protocol of 1925 and the Geneva Conventions of 1949, as well as other instruments of international law relative to respect for human rights in armed conflicts, which offer important guarantees for the protection of women and children.

4. All efforts shall be made by States involved in armed conflicts, military operations in foreign territories or military operations in territories still under colonial domination to spare women and children from the ravages of war. All the necessary steps shall be taken to ensure the prohibition of measures such as persecution, torture, punitive measures, degrading treatment and violence, particularly against that part of the civilian population that consists of women and children.

5. All forms of repression and cruel and inhuman

treatment of women and children, including imprisonment, torture, shooting, mass arrests, collective punishment, destruction of dwellings and forcible eviction, committed by belligerents in the course of military operations or in occupied territories shall be considered criminal.

6. Women and children belonging to the civilian population and finding themselves in circumstances of emergency and armed conflict in the struggle for peace, self-determination, national liberation and independence, or who live in occupied territories, shall not be deprived of shelter, food, medical aid or other inalienable rights, in accordance with the provisions of the Universal Declaration of Human Rights, the International Covenant on Civil and Political Rights, the International Covenant on Economic, Social and Cultural Rights, the Declaration of the Rights of the Child or other instruments of international law.

14

The Women 's and Children's Institutions (Licensing) Act (1956)

Act No. 105 of 1956 [30th December, 1956]

An Act to provide for the licensing of institutions for women and children and for matters incidental thereto. BE it enacted by Parliament in the Seventh Year of the Republic of India as follows:-

1. Short title, extent an commencement

(1) This Act may be called the Women's and Children's Institutions (Licensing) Act, 1956.

(2) It extends to the whole of India except the State of Jammu and Kashmir.

(3) It shall come into force in a State on such date as the State Government may, by notification in the Official Gazette, appoint.

2. Definitions

In this Act, unless the context otherwise requires:

(a) "child" means a boy or girl who has not completed the age of eighteen years;

(b) "institution" means an institution established and maintained for the reception, care, protection and welfare of women or children;

(c) "licensing authority" means the State Government or such officer or authority as may be prescribed;

(d) "prescribed" means prescribed by rules made by the State Government under this Act;

(e) "woman" means a female who has completed the age of eighteen years.

3. Licensing of institutions

After the commencement of this Act, no person shall establish or maintain an institution except under and in accordance with the conditions of a licence granted under this Act.

4. Application for licence

Every person desiring to establish an institution shall make an application to the licensing authority in such form and containing such particulars as may be prescribed:

Provided that a person maintaining an institution at the com- mencement of this Act shall be allowed a period of three months from such commencement to make an application for a licence.

5. Grant of licence

(1) On receipt of an application under section 4, the licensing authority, after making such inquiry as it considers necessary, shall, by order in writing, either grant the licence or refuse to grant it.

(2) Where a licence is refused, the grounds for such refusal shall be communicated to the applicant in the prescribed manner.

(3) A licence, unless sooner revoked, shall remain in force for such period as may be specified in the licence and may, on application made in this behalf sixty days before the date of its expiration, be renewed for such period as the licensing authority may deem proper: Provided that a licence may be renewed on an application made within sixty days before the date of its expiration if the licensing authority is satisfied that there was sufficient cause for not making the application earlier.

(4) Every licence granted under this Act shall be in the pres- cribed form and shall be subject to such conditions as may be pres- cribed: Provided that any such condition may require that the management of an institution shall, wherever practicable, be entrusted to women.

(5) No fee shall be charged for the grant of a licence under this Act.

6. Licence not transferable

A licence granted under this Act shall not be transferable.

7. Revocation of licence

(1) Where any person to whom a licence has been granted under this Act, or any agent or servant of such person commits a breach of any of the conditions thereof, or any of the provisions of this Act, or any of the rules made thereunder, or where the licensing authority is not satisfied with the condition, management or superintendence of an institution, the licensing authority may, without prejudice to any other penalty which may have been incurred under this Act, for reasons to be recorded, revoke the licence by order in writing: Provided that no such order shall be made until an opportunity is given to the holder of

the licence to show cause why the licence should not be revoked. 1233

(2) Where a licence in respect of an institution has been revoked under the foregoing sub-section, such institution shall cease to function from the date of such revocation: Provided that where an appeal lies under section 8 against the order of revocation, such institution shall cease to function:

(a) where no such appeal has been preferred, immediately on the expiration of the period prescribed for the filing of such appeal;

(b) where such appeal has been preferred but the order of revocation has been upheld, from the date of the appellate order.

(3) On the revocation of a licence in respect of an institution, the licensing authority may direct that any woman or child who is an inmate of such institution on the date of such revocation shall be- (a) restored to the custody of her or his parent, husband or lawful guardian, as the case may be; or (b) transferred to another institution.

8. Appeals

(1) Where the licensing authority is other than the State Government, any person aggrieved by an order of the licensing authority refusing to grant a licence or revoking a licence, may within such period as may be prescribed, prefer an appeal to the State Government against such refusal or revocation.

(2) The order of the State Government on such appeal and subject only to such order, the order of the licensing authority shall be final

9. Penalty

Any person who Contravenes any of the provisions of this Act or of any rule made thereunder, or any of the conditions of a licence shall be punishable with imprisonment for a term which may extend to three months, or with fine which may extend to two hundred and fifty rupees, or with both,

10. Act not to apply to certain institutions

Nothing in this Act shall apply to

(a) hostels, or boarding houses attached to, or controlled or recognised by educational institutions; or

(b) any protective home established under the Suppression of Immoral Traffic in Women and Girls Act, 1956. (104 of 1956.)

11. Power to make rules

(1) The State Government may, by notification in the Official Gazette, make rules for, carrying out the purposes of this Act. 1234

(2) In particular, and without prejudice to the generality of the foregoing power, such rules may provide for:

(a) the form of application for licence and the particulars to be contained therein;

(b) the form of licence and the conditions subject to which such licence may be granted;

(c) the management of institutions;

(d) the reception, care, protection and welfare of women and children in institutions, including all matters relating to their diet, clothing, accommodation, training and general conduct;

(e) the inspection of institutions;

(f) the maintenance of registers and account and submission of returns and audit of such accounts;

(g) the discharge from institutions of women and children and their transfer from one institution to another.

(h) the manner of filing appeals under this Act and the time within which such appeals shall be filed;

(i) the manner of service of orders and notices Under this Act;

(j) any other matter which is to be or may be prescribed.

12. Repeal and savings

(1) As from the date of commencement in any State of this Act any State Act corresponding to this Act in force in that State immediately before such commencement shall stand repealed.

(2) Notwithstanding the repeal by this Act of any State Act referred to in sub-section (1), anything done or any action taken (including any directions given, any register, rule or order made or any restriction imposed) under the provisions of such State Act shall in so far as such thing or action is not inconsistent with the provisions of this Act be deemed to have been done or taken under the provisions of this Act as if the said provisions were in force when such thing was done or such action was taken and shall continue in force accordingly until superseded by anything done or any action taken under this Act. Explanation.-In this section, the expression "State Act" in cludes a "Provincial Act". { }

15

Inter-American Convention on the Granting of Civil Rights to Women (1949)

1438 U.N.T.S. 51, entered into force *March 17, 1949*

The governments represented at the Ninth International Conference of American States,

Considering:

That the majority of the American Republics, inspired by lofty principles of justice, have granted civil rights to women;

That it has been a constant aspiration of the American community of nations to equalize the status for men and women in the enjoyment and exercise of civil rights;

That Resolution XX of the Eighth International Conference of American States expressly declares:

> "That women have the right to the enjoyment of equality as to civil status";

That long before the women of America demanded their rights they were able to carry out nobly all their responsibilities side by side with men;

That the principle of equality of human rights for men and women is contained in the Charter of the United Nations,

Have Resolved:

To authorize their respective Representatives, whose Full Powers have been found to be in good and due form, to sign the following articles:

Article 1

The American States agree to grant to women the same civil rights that men enjoy.

Article 2

The present Convention shall be open for signature by the American States and shall be ratified in accordance with their respective constitutional procedures. The original instrument, the Spanish, English, Portuguese and French texts of which are equally authentic, shall be deposited with the General Secretariat of the Organization of American States, which shall transmit certified copies to the Governments for the purpose of ratification. The instruments of ratification shall be deposited with the General Secretariat of the Organization of American States, which shall notify the signatory governments of the said deposit. Such notification shall serve as an exchange of ratifications.

Appendices

APPENDIX I

THE HUMAN RIGHTS OF WOMEN A REFERENCE GUIDE TO OFFICIAL UNITED NATIONS DOCUMENTS

CHARTER OF THE UNITED NATIONS

We the peoples of the United Nations determined to save succeeding generations from the scourge of war, which twice in our lifetime has brought untold sorrow to mankind, and to reaffirm faith in fundamental human rights, in the dignity and worth of the human person, in the equal rights of men and women and of nations large and small, and to establish conditions under which justice and respect for the obligations arising from treaties and other sources of international law can be maintained

CHAPTER I: PURPOSES AND PRINCIPLES

Article 1

The Purposes of the United Nations are:

1. To maintain international peace and security

2. To achieve international co-operation in solving international problems of an economic, social, cultural, or humanitarian character, and in promoting and encouraging respect for human rights and for fundamental freedoms for all without distinction as to race, sex, language, or religion;

Article 8

The United Nations shall place no restrictions on the eligibility of men and women to participate in any capacity and under conditions of equality in its principal and subsidiary organs.

Article 55

With a view to the creation of conditions of stability and well-being which are necessary for peaceful and friendly relations among nations based on respect for the principle of equal rights and self-determination of peoples, the United Nations shall promote:

(a) higher standards of living, full employment, and conditions of economic and social progress and development;

(b) solutions of international economic, social, health, and related problems and international cultural and educational co-operation; and

(c) universal respect for, and observance of, human rights and fundamental freedoms for all without distinction as to race, sex, language, or religion.

UNIVERSAL DECLARATION OF HUMAN RIGHTS

Preamble

Whereas recognition of the inherent dignity and of the equal and inalienable rights of all members of the human family is the foundation of freedom, justice and peace in the world,

Whereas the peoples of the United Nations have in the Charter reaffirmed their faith in fundamental human rights, in the dignity and worth of the human person and in the equal rights of men and women and have determined to promote social progress and better standards of life in larger freedom,

Article 2

Everyone is entitled to all the rights and freedoms set forth in this Declaration, without distinction of any kind, such as race, colour, sex, language, religion, political or other opinion, national or social origin, property, birth or other status.

Article 7

All are equal before the law and are entitled without any discrimination to equal protection of the law. All are entitled to equal protection against any discrimination in violation of this Declaration and against any incitement to such discrimination.

Article 16

1. Men and women of full age, without any limitation due to race, nationality or religion, have the right to marry and to found a family. They are entitled to equal rights as to marriage during marriage and at its dissolution.

2. Marriage shall be entered into only with the free and full consent of the intending spouses.

3. The family is the natural and fundamental group unit of society and is entitled to protection by society and the State.

Article 25

1. Everyone has the right to a standard of living adequate for the health and well-being of himself and of his family, including food, clothing, housing and medical care and necessary social services, and the right to security in the event of unemployment, sickness, disability, widowhood,

old age or other lack of livelihood in circumstances beyond his control.

2. Motherhood and childhood are entitled to special care and assistance. All children, whether born in or out of wedlock, shall enjoy the same social protection.

INTERNATIONAL COVENANT ON ECONOMIC, SOCIAL AND CULTURAL RIGHTS

Article 2

2. The States Parties to the present Covenant undertake to guarantee that the rights enunciated in the present Covenant will be exercised without discrimination of any kind as to race, colour, sex, language, religion, politics or other opinion, national or social origin, property, birth or other status.

Article 3

The States Parties to the present Covenant undertake to ensure the equal right of men and women to the enjoyment of all economic, social and cultural rights set forth in the present Covenant.

Article 10

The States Parties to the present Covenant recognize that:

1. The widest possible protection and assistance should be accorded to the family, which is the natural and fundamental group unit of society, particularly for its establishment and while it is responsible for the care and educate of dependent children. Marriage must be entered into with the free consent of the intending spouses.

2. Special protection should be accorded to mothers during a reasonable period before and after childbirth.

During such period working mothers should be accorded paid leave or leave with adequate social security benefits.

3. Special measures of protection and assistance should be taken on behalf of all children and young persons without any discrimination for reasons of parentage or other conditions. Children and young persons should be protected from economic and social exploitation. Their employment in work harmful to their morals or health or dangerous to life or likely to hamper their normal development should be punishable by law. States should also set age limits below which the paid employment of child labour should be prohibited and punishable by law.

Article 12

1. The States Parties to the present Covenant recognize the right of everyone to the enjoyment of the highest attainable standard of physical and mental health.

2. The steps to be taken by the States Parties to the present Covenant to achieve the full realization of this right shall include those necessary for:

(a) The provision for the reduction of the stillbirth-rate and of infant mortality and for the healthy development of the child;

INTERNATIONAL COVENANT ON CIVIL AND POLITICAL RIGHTS

Article 2

1. Each State Party to the present Covenant undertakes to respect and to ensure to all individuals within its territory and subject to its jurisdiction the rights recognized in the present Covenant, without distinction of any kind, such as race, colour, sex, language, religion, politics or other opinion, national or social origin property, birth or other status.

Article 3

The States Parties to the present Covenant undertake to ensure the equal right of men and women to the enjoyment of all civil and political rights set forth in the present Covenant.

Article 14

1. All persons shall be equal before the courts and tribunals. In the determination of any criminal charge against him, or of his rights and obligations in a suit at law, everyone shall be entitled to a fair and public hearing by a compact, independent and impartial tribunal established by law. The Press and the public may be excluded from all or part of a trial for reasons of morals, public order (*ordre public*) or national security in a democratic society, or when the interest of the private lives of the parties so requires, or to the extent strictly necessary in the opinion of the court in special circumstances where publicity would prejudice the interests of justice; but any judgement rendered in a criminal case or in a suit at law shall be made public except where the interest of juvenile persons otherwise requires or the proceedings concern matrimonial disputes or the guardianship of children.

Article 16

Everyone shall have the right to recognition everywhere as a person before the law.

Article 18

1. Everyone shall have the right to freedom of thought, conscience and religion....

4. The States Parties to the present Covenant undertake to have respect for the liberty of parents and, when applicable, legal guardians to ensure the religious and

moral education of their children in conformity with their own convictions.

Article 23

1. The family is the natural and fundamental group unit of society and is entitled to protection by society and the State.

2. The right of men and women of marriageable age to marry and to found a family shall be recognized.

3. No marriage shall be entered into without the free and full consent of the intending spouses.

4. States Parties to the present Covenant shall take appropriate steps to ensure equality of rights and responsibilities of spouses as to marriage during marriage and at its dissolution. In the case of dissolution, provision shall be made for the necessary protection of any children.

Article 24

1. Every child shall have, without any discrimination as to race, colour, sex, language, religion, national or social origin, property or birth, the right to such measures of protection as are required by his status as a minor, on the part of his family, society and the State.

2. Every child shall be registered immediately after birth and shall have a name.

3. Every child has the right to acquire nationality.

Article 26

All persons are equal before the law and are entitled without any discrimination to the equal protection of the law. In this respect, the law shall prohibit any discrimination and guarantee to all persons equal and effective protection against discrimination on any ground such as race, colour, sex, language, religion, political or other opinion, national or social origin, property, birth or other status.

APPENDIX II

NATIONAL POLICY ON EDUCATION 1986: PROGRAMME OF ACTION, GOVERNMENT OF INDIA, MINISTRY OF HUMAN RESOURCE DEVELOPMENT, DEPARTMENT OF EDUCATION, NEW DELHI

The Ministry of Human Resource Development, formulated a "National Policy on Education—1986" with the objective of giving new directions to education and to meet the challenges of new economic, social and technical development. This document was adopted by the Parliament in 1986. Consequent to this, a Programme of Action for the implementation of the new education policy was prepared with the assistance of 23 Task Forces. Each task force was assigned a specific subject covered by the National Policy on Education.

The Programme of Action has envisaged that education should be used as a strategy for achieving a basic change in the status of women. The policy placed for priority on effective universalisation of elementary education, eradication of illiteracy and skill development in the 15-35 age-group, vocationalisation of education and preparation of the manpower need for the development process, and scientific and technological research.

The recognition of the content and processes of education wee suggested along the lines of national values. Abstracts from the chapter on 'Education for Women's Equality' are enclosed.

National Policy on Education 1986: Programme of Action, Education for Women's Equality Chapter 12, Government of India, Ministry of Human Resource Development, Department of Education, New Delhi

The Present Situation

1. Provision of Educational opportunities to women has been an important programme in the education sector since independence. Between 1951 and 1981, the percentage of literacy amongst women improved from 7.93 per cent to 24.82 per cent. However, in absolute numbers, illiterate women have increased during this period from 158.7 million to 241.7 million (excluding Assam). Women comprise 57 per cent of the illiterate population and 70 per cent of the non-enrolled children of school stage are girls. In spite of the efforts made so far, the education system has not been able to make sufficient contribution towards women's equality.

Targets

(a) A phased time-bound programme of elementary education for girls, particularly upto the primary stage by 1990, and upto the elementary stage by 1995.

(b) A phased time-bound programme of adult education for women in the age-group 15-35 (whose number is estimated to be 6.8 crores) by 1995.

(c) Increased women's access to vocational, technical, professional education and to existing and emergent technologies.

(d) Review and reorganisation of the educational activities to ensure that it makes a substantial contribution towards women's equality, and creation of appropriate cells/units therefore.

Policy Parameters and Strategies

3. The National Policy on Education (NPE) envisages that education would be used as a strategy for achieving a basic change in the status of women. The National Education System would (i) play a positive interventionist role in the empowerment of women, (ii) contribute towards development of new values through redesigned curricula and text-books, and (iii) women's studies will be promoted as part of various courses. The main features of the targets and implementation strategy will consist of the following:

(i) To gear the entire education system to plan a positive interventionist role in the empowerment of women;
(ii) To promote women's studies as a part of various courses and encouragement to educational institutions to take up active programme to further women's development;
(iii) To widen the access of women in programmes of vocational, technical and professional education;
(iv) To create dynamic managerial structure to cope with the target envisaged.

STRATEGY ENUNCIATION AND PROGRAMME OF ACTION

Empowerment of Women

4. Women become empowered through collective reflection and decision-making. The parameters of empowerment are:

- Building a positive self-image and self-confidence;
- Developing ability to think critically;
- Building up group cochesion and fostering decision-making and action;

- Ensuring equal participation in the process of bringing about social change;
- Encouraging group action in order to bring about change in the society;
- Providing the wherewithal for economic independence.

5. The following measures will be taken for the achievement of the above parameters:

(a) Every educational institution should, be 1995, take up active programmes of women's development built around a study and awareness of the women's predicament and for promotion of communication and organisation among women.

(b) All teachers and non-Formal Education/Adult Education (NFE/AE) instructors should be trained as agents of women's empowerment. Special training programmes will be developed by NCERT, NIEPA, Directorate of Adult Education (DAE), SCERTs, State Resource Centres (SRCs) and UGC to incorporate in all training programmes of teachers and NFE/AE instructors elements which would motivate them to work for women's empowerment. Voluntary agencies and activist groups for women's development will be involved in these training programmes.

(c) Women teachers and women instructors in adult/non-formal education programmes should receive special orientation to enable them to play an activist role towards women's equality.

(d) Special programmes should be developed by research institutions, voluntary institutions and professional groups of artists to promote general awareness and self-image amongst women through a variety of programmes like discussions, street plays, skits, wall papers, puppet shows etc.

(e) An environment should be created in which practically all sections of the society will commit themselves an work for achieving this objective enunciated in the National Policy on Education. Keeping in view the important role played by media in this sphere, clear policy guidelines should be developed by radio and TV in 1986-87 and measures taken to persuade films and other media on these lines.

(f) Preference in recruitment of teachers upto school level should be for women. This will create a greater confidence in the rural areas and motivate the parents to send girls to the school.

(g) The common core curriculum is a powerful instrument for the empowerment of women through the incorporation of values commensurate with the new status of women. The Women's Cell in the NCERT will be revived and given the responsibility for preparing the component of the core curriculum relating to women's equality. The Cell should also accelerate its work of eliminating sexist bias and sex stereotypes from school text-books. The Women's Cell of NCERT should take active help of all persons on playing its assigned role.

(h) Sensitisation of teachers, trainers, planners and administrators to women's issues will be taken up as a major programme by NIEPA and appropriate State level agencies, through initial training, in-service training and refresher courses.

NIEPA should also have a strong cell for planning and execution of these programmes.

Women Studies

6. Women's studies programme has 4 dimensions—teaching, research, training and extension. In teaching the following activities will be taken up:

(i) Incorporation of issues fating to women's status and role in the foundation course proposed to be introduced by University Grants Commission for all undergraduate students;
(ii) Incorporation of the women's dimension into courses in different disciplines;
(iii) Elimination of sexist bias and sex stereo-types from text books.

7. Under research, the following steps will be taken

(i) Encouraging research on identified areas and subjects which are crucial in advancing knowledge in this area and expand the information base;
(ii) Critical appraisal of existing tools and techniques which have been responsible for the disadvantages suffered by them and where necessary reformation of research methodology.

8. The following measures will be taken under training:

(i) Dissemination of information and interaction through seminars/workshops on the need for Women's Studies and its role in University education;
(ii) Orientation of teachers and researchers to handle women-related topics and to incorporate women's dimension into general topics;

(iii) Workshops for restructuring the curriculum.

9. Under extension, it is proposed to encourage educational institutions to take up programmes which directly benefit the community and bring about the empowerment of women.

10. These would include actual implementation of development programmes directly aimed at women's empowerment such as adult education, awareness building, legal literacy, informational and training support for socio-economic programmes of women's development, media, etc.

Universalisation of Elementary Education and Adult Education

11. The present programme of non-formal centres for girls on 90:10 pattern will be extended to all educationally backward pockets of the country. NEF Centres should be community based. Responsibility of planning, selection of instructors and monitoring should be with the community including parents. Increased assistance to voluntary agencies to run nonformal education centres for girls should be given.

12. In the rural areas, girls are kept busy at home in sibling and household care, in fetching fuel, fodder and water, or in earning a day's wage. Therefore, special support services referred to in the Policy need to cover all these areas upto 1995. Early childhood education centres are important support service in increasing enrolment and retention of girls in schools. Programmes of social forestry, drinking water supply, mid-day meals, and other nutrition programmes, smokeless chullahas and other devices aimed at eliminating drudgery from women's lives should be formulated by the Ministry and organisation concerned

upto 1990 to converge with the objective of universalisation of education.

13. Skill development linked to employment or work opportunities in the villages or local areas are required to be given overriding priority so that there is an incentive on the part of the parents to educate the girls.

14. Mass scale adult education programmes for women in the age-group 15-35 should be developed to eradicate illiteracy amongst women by 1995. As majority of women in this age-group are workers literacy per se may not have any relevance for them. It is, therefore, necessary to develop adult education programmes for women linked with upgradation of their skills and income generating activities.

15. Skill development for girls and women should be continuous process of learning starting from the NFE centres and AE centres. Continuing Education Centres should be set up in a phased manner which should organise vocational training, provide opportunities for retention of literacy skills and application of this learning for improving their living conditions.

16. The skill development given by the Continuing Education Centres will be supported by other programmes of nonformal, vocational training and skill development to be administered by a variety of organisations and institutions, such as Polytechnics, Community Polytechnics, ITIs, Shramik Vidyapeeths, Central Social Welfare Board, State Social Welfare Advisory Boards, Voluntary Agencies, Krishi Vigyan Kendras, Women's Centres in Agricultural and Home Science Colleges as part of their extension activities. Besides, industries which employ women should themselves run non-formal vocational training courses.

For effective learning and monitoring Women's Bureau is to be set up in the Department of Education.

Women's Access to Vocational, Technical and Professional Education and to Existing and Emergent Technologies

17. At each stage in school education; or a part of work experience or vocationalisation, girls should be exposed to a variety of vocational training activities. The method of vocational training should be both through the formal and non-formal courses. The choice of skills to be taught will depend on the natural resources, traditional occupations and new activities being taken up through government and private investment.

18. There are 104 ITIs functioning exclusively for women and 97 wings in general ITIs reserved for women. It is proposed that these institutions be revamped during the period 1987-90 on the following lines:

(i) Diversification of trades and courses, will be done, keeping the job potential of the area in mind. There will be an efficient placement system which will enable the institutions to have continuous dialogue with employers. The idea behind this diversification is that while girls will continue to receive preferential treatment in trades/occupations, for which they are particularly well suited (e.g. teaching and nursing), this will not become a barrier for their participation in technical and professional courses of higher level and equal opportunities will be provided for them in all vocational, technical and professional courses.

(ii) There will be a strong element of vocational counselling in each ITI/RVTI/NVTI, polytechnics. Suitable orientation should also be provided in the schools as preparation for motivating the girls to choose non-traditional courses.

(iii) Information about credit, banking, entrepreneurial development etc. will be provided by the ITI/NVTI/RVTI/polytechnics and community polytechnics alongwith practical on-the-job training. The implementation of the apprenticeship scheme will be strengthened to increase the coverage of women.

(iv) In order to substantially enlarge the opportunities to women for craftsmen's training, sift system will be introduced in existing ITIs—one in the morning and the other in the afternoon.

(v) DGE&T office should have a separate Directorate of Women's Vocational Training.

(vi) The women's access to technical education will be improved qualitatively and quantitatively. The choice of traders/displines offered to women at Certificate/Diploma/Degree levels in all types of technical education institutions, will be made keeping in view the objective of bringing about women's equality. Necessary incentives, as spelt out in the section of Technical Education will be provided.

Management Structure at Centre and State Level

19. The interventions and programmes referred to above will be planned, coordinated, monitored and evaluated continuously both at the national and state level. Each of the organisations responsible for the programme will have to be strengthened. The Women's Cell in the NCERT will

be revived and strengthened. NIEPA and Directorate of Adult Education will have strong cells to plan and administer Women's training programmes. The Women's Cell in the UGC will be strengthened in order to monitor the implementation of various programmes at higher education level.

20. At the the State level, Women's Cell should be set up in all the State with adequate supporting staff to be headed by an officer of at least Joint Director's status.

APPENDIX III

DECLARATION OF MEXICO PLANS OF ACTION. WORLD CONFERENCE OF THE INTERNATIONAL WOMEN'S YEAR, 19 JUNE—2 JULY, 1975. UNITED NATIONS, DECEMBER, 1975

In order to eliminate all obstacles that stand in the way of enjoyment by women of equal status with men, the Mexico plans of Action decided to promulgate 30 principles on the equality of women and their contribution to national development and international peace. For imlementation purposes, the objectives of the Mexico Plans of Action were divided into two categories—the World Plan of Action and the Regional Plans of Action. The main purpose was to stimulate national, international and regional action to solve the problems of underdevelopment and of the socio-economic structure which place women in an inferior position.

The major highlights of the Mexico Plans of Action were the 14 minimum objectives to be achieved by member countries by the end of the first five year period (1975-1980) of the UN decade for Women. These objectives were:

1. Marked increase in literacy and civic education of women, especially rural areas;

2. The extension of co-educational, technical and vocational training in basic skills to women and men in the industrial and agricultural sectors;
3. Equal access at every level of education, compulsory primary school education and the measures necessary to prevent school drops-outs;
4. Increased employment opportunities for women, reduction of unemployment and increased efforts to eliminate discrimination in the terms and conditions of employment;
5. The establishment and increase in the infrastructural services, required in both rural and urban areas;
6. The enactment of legislation on voting and eligibility for election on equal terms with men, equal opportunity and conditions of employment including remuneration, and on equality in legal capacity and the exercise thereof;
7. Encouragement of a greater participation of women in policy making positions at the local, national and international levels;
8. Increased provision for comprehensive measures for health education and services, sanitation, nutrition, family education, family planning and other welfare services;
9. Provision of parity in the exercise of civil, social and political rights such as those pertaining to marriage, citizenship and commerce;
10. Recognition of the economic value of women's work in the home, in domestic food production and marketing of voluntary activities not remunerated;

11. The direction of formal, non-formal and life-long education towards the re-evaluation of the men and women, in order to ensure their full realisation as an individuals in the families and in society;
12. The promotion of women's organisations as an interim measure within workers' organisations and educational, economic and professional institutions;
13. The development of modern rural technology, cottage industry, pre-school day centres, time-and-energy-saving devices so as to help reduce the heavy work load of women, particularly those living in rural sectors and for the urban poor and thus facilitate the full participation of women in community, national and international affairs;
14. The establishment of interdisciplinary and multisectoral machinery within the Government for accelerating the achievement of equal opportunities for women and their full integration into national life.

Convention on the Elimination of all Forms of Discrimination Against Women

United Nations 1975

The 30 article Convention calls for equal rights for women, regardless of their marital status, in all fields—political, economic, social, cultural and civil. It calls for national legislation to ban discrimination; recommends temporary special measure to speed equality between men and women; and action to modify social and cultural patterns that perpetuate discrimination.

Other measures provide for equal rights for women in political and public life; equal access to education and same choice of curricula; nondiscrimination in employment and pay; and guarantees of job security in the event of marriage and maternity. The convention underlines the equal responsibilities of men and women in the context of family life. It also stresses the social services needed—especially child care facilities, for combining family obligations with work responsibilities and participation in public life. The Committee on the Elimination of Discrimination Against Women (CEDAW), monitors progress made in implementation of the Convention.

By 31 May 1987, 93 countries had consented to be bound by the provisions of the Convention, either through ratification or accession. India has signed the convention but has not ratified it.

Programme of Action for the Second Half of the United Nations Decade for Women: Equality, Development and Peace. World Conference, Copenhagen, 14-30 July 1980, Government of India, Ministry of Social Welfare, Women's Welfare and Development Bureau, New Delhi.

The General Assembly resolution of 1975 decided that in 1980, at the mid-point of the Decade, a world conference of the UN Decade for Women would be convened. The purposes were two fold: (i) to review and evaluate progress made by member countries in implementing the recommendations of the World Conference of the International Women's Year held in 1975, and (ii) to readjust programmes for the second half of the Decade in the light of new data and research. This report, prepared by the Government of India, consists of three parts.

Part one outlines the historical background and

conceptual framework of the Programme of Action. Part two consists of Programme of Action at the National Level. These include national strategies for accelerating the full participation of women in economic and social development; objectives and priority areas for action taken in connection with the subtheme of the world conference. Part three consists of the Programmes of Action at the International and Regional Levels.

Some priority areas requiring special attention were identified. These included food production, problems of rural women, provision of child care services, problems of migrant women, unemployed women, young women and women who alone are responsible for their families.

India—A Status Paper. World Conference of the U.N. Decade for Women 14-30 July, 1980, Government of India, Ministry of Social Welfare, 1980.

Para 46 of the World Plan of Action adopted by the World Conference of the International Women's Year, outlined 14 minimum objectives to be achieved by the end of the first half of the U.N. Decade for Women, i.e. 1975—1980. This paper was prepared in 1980 by the Ministry of Social Welfare, Government of India in an attempt to review India's progress in attaining those minimum objectives. Various initiatives undertaken by the Government of India were highlighted.

The review also indicated the constraints and problems faced in promoting participation of women in development and in improving their status. The document pointed to the fact it had been possible to provide for de jure equality, services and facilities for education, health care and training of women. But due to the effect of traditional constraints and attitudes, increasing affirmative action was required in favour of women to convert de jure equality into de facto equality.

Report of the Regional Intergovernmental Preparatory Meeting for the World Conference to Review and Appraise the Achievements of the United Nations Decade for Women: Equality, Development and Peace. United Nations Economics and Social Commission for Asia and the Pacific, Tokyo, 26-30 March, 1984.

Representatives from member countries and various organisations met in 1984 to review and appraise the achievements of the subtheme of United Nations Decade for Women: Equality, Development and Peace. It was noted that due to a growing recognition of the critical importance of integrating women into national socio-economic policies and plans, there had been some progress. But due to compartmentalisation of women's issues the progress has been unsatisfactory—being unequally distributed, isolated and fragmentary in nature. Impediments to effective planning and plan implementation included the lack of an adequate resource base in terms of trained personnel, finance and inappropriate data. Forward looking strategies were designed. It was suggested that these strategies, should address these continuing concerns in a more effective manner so that women are recognised as productive contributions to development and its beneficiaries. To achieve these goals, it was also suggested to mobilise national and legislative machinery as well as promote a high degree of public awareness of women's contribution to national development. The other major obstacle highlighted was pervasiveness of social attitudes deep-rooted in tradition and history.

New Delhi Document on Women in Development: Conference of Non-Aligned and other Developing Countries on the Role of Women in Development, New Delhi, 10-11 April, 1985.

The delegates examined in depth the role of women in developing countries, areas of cooperation exchange of expertise and shared experiences, in light of preparations for the World Conference. The intention was to approach the World Conference with full knowledge to their achievements and failures, and to evolve a strategy to tackle the problems confronting the world.

The current status of women was reviewed and appraised in the context of various sectors such as agriculture, food production, rural development, industrialisation, education, mass media, science and technology, population, housing and environmental issues. Problem areas and obstacles in attaining the objectives of the UN Decade for Women were identified. One of the basic obstacles in achieving women's equality was the non-recognition of women's pivotal role in society. Lack of concerted and determined efforts to remove gender-bias was recognised as the second important obstacle. Thirdly project planning seemed to pay scant attention to the linkages between women's productive and reproductive work. Usually, programmes or projects focussed on only one or the other aspect. Hence the need for a more "holistic" view of women's work and contribution was emphasised. New approaches and forward looking strategies to achieve the objectives of the UN Decade were designed:

Forward Looking Strategies for the Advancement of Women. The World Conference to Review and Appraise the Achievements of the UN Decade for Women: Equally, Developments and Peace. Nairobi (Kenya), 15-26 July, 1985. Government of India, Ministry of Human Resource Development, Department of Women's Welfare, New Delhi.

The Forward Looking Strategies (FLS) for the Advancement of Women from 1986 to the year 2000 was adopted at the UN Decade for Women World Conference held in Nairobi, Kenya, in July 1985. They were built on the earlier world conference on women, on the work of the UN Commission on the status of women and on the activities and ideas of the world wide women's movement. These strategies were designed to serve as guidelines for creating a new world order based on equality, development and peace. Some of the measures were intended to affect women directly. Others were designed to make the societal context less obstructive and more supportive of their progress such as the elimination of sex-based stereotypes.

Women in India-Country Paper 1985. Government of India, Ministry of Social and Women's Welfare, New Delhi.

At the end of the UN Decade for Women, a country paper was prepared by the Ministry of Social Welfare, Government of India. The purpose was to identify areas in which work has been done to improve the status of women. The paper highlighted the developments with regard to demography, law, employment, health, education, political participation, family, science and technology and institutional arrangements. It also outlined the obstacles and bottlenecks in each areas and suggested modifications and strategies to improve the situation.

Women in Development: Report of SAARC Ministerial Meeting. Shillong, May 6-8, 1986. Government of India, Ministry of Human Resource Development, Department of Women and Child Development, New Delhi.

In pursuance of the decision taken at the first Summit of the Heads of State or Government of the South Asian Association for Regional Cooperation held at Dhaka in

December 1985, two meetings took place. The first Ministerial meeting on Women in Development was held at Shillong on May 6-8, 1986 at the invitation of the Government of India. The second official level meeting on Women in Development was held in New Delhi on April 8-10, 1986. The basic objectives were to promote the welfare of the peoples of South Asia and to improve their quality of life. This meeting reflected their conviction that no meaningful progress could be achieved without the active participation of women and the enhancement of the status of women who form half the populating in this region.

At the Ministerial Meeting the ministers reviewed the overall situation of women in the South Asian countries and noted that considerable progress has been achieved in several social sectors affecting women. However, greater attention was still required to be focussed on critical areas. Some of these were the low level of literacy, poor enrolment in schools coupled with high drop out rates; lack of vocational and technical training, marketing and credit facilities; the low level of political participation and involvement in policy making and its implementation. It was felt that special efforts were also required to disseminate appropriate technologies to eliminate drudgery and thus improve the quality of life of women particularly in the rural areas.

At the Official Level Meeting, delegates from each member country presented General Statements on the issues pertaining to Women in Development and high-lighted major achievements as also major problems being faced by them. The basic categories included women's access to basic needs, women and environment, family welfare, access to employment, their participation in the development process and cooperation among NGOs. It was suggested that the exchange of training and consultancy services and personnel in the countries of the region was found to be inadequate and steps were needed to compile such information.

APPENDIX IV

SEVENTH FIVE YEAR PLAN 1985-90: SOCIO-ECONOMIC PROGRAMMES FOR WOMEN

CHAPTER 17. GOVERNMENT OF INDIA, PLANNING COMMISSION, NEW DELHI

Background

The Constitution of India provides for equal rights and privileges for men and women and makes special provisions for women to help them improve their status in society. A number of social enactments have been put on the statute books for removing various constraints which hindered their progress. In spite of these measures, women have lagged behind men in different spheres, especially in education. The female literacy rate has consistently been lower in rural as well as urban sectors. In rural areas, where 77 per cent of the female population lives, women's literacy rate is only 17.96 per cent. The urban literacy rate for females is 47.82 per cent. The literacy rate for females varies from 65.73 per cent in Kerala to only 11.42 per cent in Rajasthan. There are many reasons for this generally of sociological nature.

The health problem of women in society at large is another crucial area not given the required attention. Due to the predominantly patriarchal order, women are confined within an oppressive environment. Differences are frequently noted between health and nutritional status of men and women. Nutritional surveys have indicated high rates of inadequacies among females compared to males. Female infants and children are subject to neglect in respect of nutrition and health care. Statistics from primary health centres show that adult women do not generally take treatment from them. Maternal mortality continues to be very high. A number of studies have indicated that a large number of children suffer from malnutrition to which the mother's poor health contributes to a great extent. Anaemia among rural women is estimated to be as high as 60-80 per cent, leading to low birth weight among babies.

According to the 1981 Census only 14 per cent of the total female population in the country fall in the category of "workers." The unpaid economic activities of women and their contribution through work in the domestic sectors remain unreported in the census. An ILO study has estimated that the value of unpaid household work constitutes 25-39 per cent of the total gross national product in developing countries.

Women play an important role in agricultural production, animal husbandry and other related activities such as storage, marketing of produce, food processing etc. Apart from these, they spend almost 10-12 hours per day doing household chores including fetching of water and gathering of fuel. Large number of female labourers are engaged in the plantation sector. About 54 per cent of rural women and 26 per cent of urban women are engaged in marginal occupations in order to supplement the family income by collection of fish, small game, firewood, cow-dung, maintenance of kitchen gardens, tailoring, weaving and teaching but the quantification of this activity, in terms of work-hours contributed, or its income generating equivalent was not attempted or recorded.

Recently a declining trend has been observed in the employment of women labourers. Some of the new technologies have displaced women from many of the traditional activities. The incomes of the poor households are supplemented by women, although they have to face many problems due to family responsibilities, limited mobility and social restrictions. The Green Revolution has led to increased demands for casual labour dispossession of small landholders from their land and consequently, pushing out of women from such small landholding to become wage earners. Though many of the tasks performed by males are getting mechanised, the women continue to toil in labour intensive jobs like rice transplantation, cleaning and storage of grain in post-harvest operations, picking of leaves and fruit, handshelling groundnut, picking out common-seed etc. Women get limited job opportunities in modern occupations/trades as they do not have access to the training required for new technologies. In Many areas where multiple crops are grown, the workload of women has increased. In industry women continue to be employed mostly on unskilled jobs. The average earning of a regular salaried woman worker continues to be less than that of a man.

An emerging phenomenon in the rural scene is the "single parent rural family," due to large scale migration of men seeking employment in urban areas. The women has to assume the role of head of the household and responsibility for the support and care of children and also of the elders in the rural family. Her income is income is inadequate to meet the family needs. Thus, there is tension in the family as remittances from the men-folk are mostly irregular as also meagre, given the high cost (and many temptations) of urban living.

There is considerable evidence to show that parents discriminate against girls in the matter of science education.

With the majority of women being engaged in agriculture and allied fields an exposure to science and technology aimed at, and for the benefit of women, has yet to come about. There is a felt need to structure courses, through visual as well as other (literacy-based) media, which are related to health and health care, nutrition (especially of young children), simple-to follow techniques against morbidity (especially from water-borne infections) and infant mortality (e.g. oral rehydration therapy), food preservation and enrichment and for a balanced diet using readily available natural foods and additives. Inputs of science and technology are required also in housing cooking and performance of other household work, which can lead to a considerable reduction in drudgery. Time and energy thus saved could be used by rural women for improvement of their knowledge, skill and aptitude levels.

There has been, in general a lack of awareness among the people about various legislations and programmes being implemented for the benefit of women. Although the socio-cultural situation, to a great extent keeps women isolated, lately the radio, TV and other mass communication media have exposed them to information and knowledge. However, such exposure has not yet resulted in creating consciousness to the desired extent among women nor has it succeeded in loosening the hold of tradition oriented thinking and mores. The significant role that is rightly women's in such vital areas as attitudes to education, health and health care as well as nutrition and related delivery system reduction of infant mortality; in meaningful participation in many skilled jobs in advanced science and technology areas like medicine and medical research, electronics and informatics, education and teaching, energy conservation and in improving the quality of life, has not yet been grasped fully by society at large.

Sixth Plan Review

During the Sixth Plan, a variety of programmes were taken up under different sectors of development to ameliorate the working conditions of women and to raise their economic and social status.

A special cell created in 1976 continued to look after the employment of women and monitor the implementation of the equal Remuneration Act, enacted to provide for wages equal to those of men for work of similar nature. Three regional vocational training centres one each at Bangalore, Bombay and Trivandrum, and a National Vocational Training Institute at New Delhi, with a total annual intake capacity of 600 women trainees, were set up by the Directorate General of Employment and Training (DGE and T). A part from these 144 Industrial Training Institutes (ITIs) exclusively meant for women were functioning in different States by the end of the Sixth Plan. The intake capacity in these institutions is 11.200 per annum.

In the Rural Development Sector, the Integrated Rural Development Programme (IRDP) accorded priority to women heads of households. On the whole women comprised 7 per cent of the beneficiaries covered under the IRDP during the Sixth Plan. A decision was also taken that a minimum of one-third of the beneficiaries under TRYSEM would be women and thereby about 3.27 lakh women constituting 34.8 per cent of the total number of beneficiaries were trained. A new scheme, namely "Development of Women and Children in Rural Areas" (DWCRA) was started in 1982-83 as a pilot project in 50 blocks of the country. Women who were not in a position to take advantage of scheme under the IRDP Programme were organised into homogeneous groups of 15 to 20. Each such group was provided training in a chosen economic activity along with necessary infrastructure. Such activities included weaving, fish vending, broom and rope making, brick making and pickle making. Training was also given in candle making and in banking. The scheme has proved quite popular. Over 1900 groups were formed and trained, benefiting about 30,000 women during the two-year period, 1983-85.

The scheme of Krishi Vigyan Kendras introduced for bridging the gap between the farmer's knowledge and available technology also covered women. Eight home science, colleges for women attached to agricultural universities were set up to provide training and research facilities.

A radical move in the concerted attempt to improve women's status was the decision to confer join titles on husband and wife in all development activities involving transfer of assets distribution of land and house sites.

In order to encourage girls into elementary and higher education, a Centrally sponsored scheme was taken up for providing financial assistance to educationally-backward States for establishing non-formal education centres exclusively for girls. Financial assistance was given for appointment of women teachers in primary schools. Incentives were provided to State at different administrative levels for encouraging girls to enrol in larger numbers. Text-books for elementary and high schools were evaluated with a view to vocationalising higher education.

Nearly 73 per cent of the total non-enrolled children in the 6-11 years age-group were girls. In the age-group 11-14 years, only 38 per cent of girls had been enrolled for formal education. The drop-out rate of girls both at the elementary and secondary levels of education continues to be high. To boost enrolment in the primary classes, early childhood education centres for children in the age-group 3-6 years were set up as adjuncts to primary schools for the first time in the Sixth Five Year Plan in rural and backward areas. These centres also provided creche facilities for younger siblings of girls attending primary schools. The scheduled caste/scheduled tribe girls continued to receive higher rates of post matric scholarship as compared to boys. Other incentives to girls included free clothing and free tuition. To give additional fillip to higher education among women, separate universities for women have been established in the States of Tamil Nadu and Andhra Pradesh.

Special programmes were taken up for women in adult education centres, providing education in subjects like health, nutrition, child care and family planning. The curriculum also included skills like teaching, sewing, embroidery and building up of awareness and functionality through discussions and literature. The enrolment of women under the Adult Education Programme in December, 1984 was reported 2.89 million, the coverage being about 52 per cent of the total enrolment. Besides, 4,62,000 women were also covered under the programme "Functional Literacy of Adult Women," implemented by the Ministry of Social Welfare.

Under the scheme 'Science and Technology for Women' a wide spectrum of activities was taken up. Projects were sponsored for development of smokless chullahs, use of solar cookers, setting up bio-gas plants, and devices for improving the water purification system. New programmes which had a bearing on the overall economic development of women and reduction in their drudgery have been identified, such as improved agricultural implements for farming in hill areas, better methods of sheep-rearing and wool-spinning devices for women. Several technologies were developed in the areas of transplantation, post harvest activities, fish-cum-paddy culture, processing of rice products, fish processing, pearl culture and in the cashew and coir industry. Research and development activities were taken up to minimise physical discomfort to orthopaedically handicapped women while working on handlooms.

Added impetus was given to the training of women instrumentation technology for repair and maintenance of electronic equipments in offices and hospitals. In certain areas of West Bengal, tribal women were trained in making blocks from stone chips, in bamboo craft and rope making in Maharashtra. With a view to training women in identification of herbs of medicinal value and cultivation and preparation of standardised medicinal formulations, experiments were conducted on vegetable gardening in courtyards and on rooftops. Studies were undertaken to assess the incidence of bronchial asthma and skin diseases amongst women engaged in sericulture.

A report was brought out on "Organisational and Environmental Health Problems of Indian Women," containing detailed information on the health hazards to women in different occupations. Also, a film, "Science and Technology for Women," is under preparation.

A number of technology demonstration-cum-training centres at selected focal points all over the country were set up by National Research Development Corporation (NRDC) to provide expertise and resources to women entrepreneures in respect of new technologies relevant to their daily needs and economic enterprises. Low-cost industrial technologies were also developed, relating to food products, post-harvest operation, domestic aids for pure drinking water, educational toys, low-cost latrines and improved chullahs. A number of projects on agro-waste compaction, machines for converting agricultural waste into fuel and other technologies relating to food, chemicals, drugs and pharmaceuticals, energy and fuel, building materials, were taken up by NRDC. A compendium on appropriate technologies for women developed by NRDC was also published.

A major step was taken by the University Grants Commission (UGC) to provide a boost to women's participation in the field of science and technology by enhancing by 10 years the age of eligibility for women scientists to receive research fellowships.

Various measures have been taken to improve women's health and nutritional status. Nutritional intervention to the most vulnerable group of women, namely, pregnant and nursing mothers belonging to the weaker sections, was given high priority. Under the Integrated Child Development Services (ICDS), special nutrition was provided to pregnant women and nursing mothers. At the end of the Sixth Plans, more than 1.2 million such women were receiving benefits under the programme.

Provision was made for expanding maternal and child health (MCH) programmes including training of local dais. In order to induct local women as auxiliary nurse-midwives (ANMs), the educational qualifications for their training were relaxed to the seventh standard if girls with requisite educational qualifications at the higher level were not available. The upper age limit of training for ANMS was also raised. Prophylaxis programmes against nutritional anaemia of pregnant and lactating mothers were implemented. Iron and folic acid tablets were distributed to more than 72.5 million pregnant women and nursing mothers. Tetanus Toxoid was administered to about 36 million pregnant women.

Under the family welfare programme, the couple protection rate was expected to have reached 36.6 per cent by the end of March 1985. It is worth mentioning that the female infant mortality rate had fallen from 148 in 1972 to 115 in 1980, where as the male infant mortality rate fell from 132 in 1972 to 113 in 1980. The fall in mortality rate of female infants has been more rapid as compared to males. However, the rate of infant mortality is still too high (through there are considerable inter-State differences) and needs to be reduced drastically. The sex ratio which had presistently been declining upto 1971 had shown a slight rise in 1981. In the 1971 Census, the sex ratio was recorded as 930, but this rose to 933 in the 1981 Census. The maternal mortality rate of 4.17 per thousand live births during 1980 continued to be disturbingly high.

A number of schemes were taken up in the social welfare sector to benefit destitute and needy women. By the end of 1984-85, voluntary organisations were assisted in the construction of 344 hostels for working women. Nearly 3000 women were given training in skills in modern industries and provided employment under the scheme 'Employment and Income-Generating Training-cum-Oroduction Centres for Women'. Condensed courses of education and vocational training courses were organised by a number of voluntary organisations benefiting 1,11,000 women. Under the 'socio-economic programme' 3589 units were sanctioned, with a coverage of 47,011 women. The scheme of "Assistance to women in distress" covered only 9,260 women through 267 vocational courses in non-traditional trades with the aim of making these women economically independent.

For creating increasing awareness of the role of women in development and the need for improvement of their status, various media units under the Ministry of Information and Broadcasting presented appealing programmes on social and economic problems and other related issues faced by women.

To mould public opinion against atrocities on women, a number of interviews and discussions were held with legal experts, social workers and officials of women's organisations. All India Radio in collaboration with different State Governments and assisted by UNICEF, organised twelve radio workshops on maternity and child care. The various Doordarshan Kendras also included in their programmes messages pertaining to the status of women. Audience programmes for rural people and industrial workers were also telecast. The Press Information Bureau took up a programme of mass education and information to promote positive social attitudes towards women and motivate people to fight social evils like dowry, child marriage, drinking, etc. A booklet entitled 'Status of Women' was published by the Directorate of Field Publicity. The Song and Drama Division of AIR took up programmes for women's upliftment. The Film and Television Institute of India prepared programmes highlighting women's problems and development schemes for them.

Seventh Plan: Objective and Strategies

The long-term objectives of the developmental programmes for women would be to raise their economic and social status in order to bring them into the mainstream of national development. Due recognition has to be accorded to the role and contribution of women in the various socio-economic, political and cultural activities.

In the Seventh Plan, the basic approach would be to inculate confidence among women and bring about an awareness of their own potential for development, as also of their rights and privileges. The various mass communication media would be utilised extensively in this task. Special measures would be initiated for strict enforcement of the Dowry Prohibition Act and also to prevent harassment and atrocities on women. Voluntary agencies and educational institutions would be fully involved in launching organised campaigns to combat these evils. An integrated multi-disciplinary approach would be adopted covering employment, education, health, nutrition, application of science and technology and other related aspects in areas of interest to women. Efforts would be made to extend facilities for income-generating activities and to enable women to participate actively in socio-economic development. The educational programmes will be restructured and the school curricula will be modified to eliminate gender bias. Enrolment of girls in elementary, higher secondary and higher education courses, formal as well as non-formal, will be given high priority.

In the field of science and technology stress would be laid on evolving devises to reduce the drudgery of women so that the time saved is utilised for development activities. Training and retraining would be ensured for many S and T related programmes. The beneficiary-oriented programmes in the various sectors of development would be suitably modified on re-oriented so that the due share of benefits from such programmes is availed by them.

Collation and analysis of information and relevant data on the development programmes for women will be undertaken in an effective manner.

Major Programmes

Education: During the Seventh Plan, sustained efforts, through various schemes and measures, would have to be made in order to reach 100 per cent coverage in elementary education, for children upto the age of 14 years. The Schemes of "Financial Assistance to Voluntary Agencies to run early childhood education (pre-school) centres as adjuncts of primary/middle schools" would be expanded, particularly to evolve innovative models suited to specific learner groups or areas. The programme would receive greater attention in all the ICDS blocks. Educational campaigns for tackling the prejudices and socio religious constraints would be taken up on a wider scale since nearly three-fourths of the out-of-school children are girls. Efforts would be made to enrol and retain girls in school, especially in rural areas and for children belonging to scheduled castes, scheduled tribes and other weaker sections. At the elementary stages, education has been made free for girls in all States/UTs. Priority would continue to be given to women in teachers training programmes to increased the availability of trained women teachers and thereby to enhance girls enrolment and retention in schools. Incentives like uniforms, free textbooks and attendance scholarships would be continued to the needy girls in all schools.

Non-formal elementary education would be expanded to benefit girls in the age-group 6-14 years.

Under the Adult Education Programme, apart from increasing the coverage, the educational content of the programme would be modified to incorporate new value systems in the community regarding the role of women in the family and community.

The Seventh Plan envisages, among other schemes

the preparation of district level plans as a mass movement with local community participation both for activising and implementing the literacy programmes, and the creation of special mechanisms to monitor the progress of implementation at State level. Integrated Rural Development Programme (IRDP), National Rural Employment Programme (NREP), Training of Rural Youth in Self-Employment (TRYSEM) and other such programmes would have a component of functional literacy for women beneficiaries.

Talented girls would be encouraged to pursue higher education. It is also proposed to expand the "Open Learn Systems", including correspondence courses for them.

In order to promote technical and vocational education for girls, more women's polytechnics would be up and programmes for vocationalisation of education would be expanded.

To boost education among the girls of the scheduled castes and scheduled tribes, additional facilities would continue to be provided under the "Development of Backward Classes" sector. Girls above the matriculation stage would get higher scholarships stipends than those for the boy students. Financial assistance is envisaged for construction of hostel buildings for girls at district level and for purchase of equipment furniture, utensils, books and periodicals in these hostels.

Under the National Sports Policy, participation of women and girls in sports and games would be encouraged. Stress would be laid on the identification of sports talent among women and provision made for sports, scholarships, coaching and nourishment support for promising girls with a view to increase standards of their performance in competitive games. Besides, schemes for encouraging traditional folk, tribal and hill arts and cultural activities would be expanded and strengthened.

Health: Under the Health Sector, the major thrust during the next ten years will be directed towards the reduction of the prevailing high maternal and infant mortality rates. For this purpose emphasis will be placed on the expansion of MCH care which will give considerable importance to preventive promotive and educational services. Specifically schemes for giving tetanus toxoid to mothers and providing proper ante-natal care will be taken up on a sizeable scale. Besides close linkages with other related sectors will be established in order to make a dent on the problem. The health and family welfare services will be made available to all women in the reproductive age-group. The existing bed strengths at the district hospitals would be augmented and a sizeable proportion of them would be allocated to women and children. The health sub-centre coverage for providing health services would be progressively reduced to below 5000 persons per sub-centre. Besides, nutrition supplements iron and folic acid tablets would be given to mothers for bridging the calorie-vitamin and mineral deficiency gap as well as for fighting anaemia. The scheme for training of birth attendants and auxiliary nurse midwives would be expanded considerably. Efforts would be made to promote health consciousness, so that the available health infrastructure could be fully utilised. Mass media, voluntary agencies, village health committees, women's organisations and dais will be employed to spread knowledge about simple remedies for common disorders. Women would also be informed about misleading advertisements regarding the use of tonics, health drinks, etc. Knowledge about the nutritional status of girls and its impact on the health and weight of the babies born would be disseminated widely.

Such published information would include the demographic and socio-cultural implications of the present adverse sex ratio and low age at marriage will be publicised.

Employment

(i) *Agriculture and allied sectors:* Special attention would be given to improving existing skills of women and imparting to them new skills under the programmes of farmers' training, exchange of development, fodder production, post-harvest technology, application of pesticides, budding and grafting, farmers training in horticulture, fisheries, poultry, dairy, social forestry etc. Horticultural research and development programmes would play a significant role in economic and nutritional progress particularly with respect to the problem of under-nutrition of pregnant women and nursing mothers and their children.

(ii) *Rural development:* The Integrated Rural Development Programme meant for the poorest in the rural areas, has been formulated for creating assets with a view to increasing the productivity and income-generation ability of the beneficiaries in a specified period of time. The programme has been extended to all the 5092 development blocks in the country during the Sixth Plan. About 20 million beneficiaries would be covered during the Seventh Plan. This would include 50 per cent of the old beneficiaries who may require a second dose of assistance at an average rate of Rs. 500. The new beneficiaries however, would receive an enhanced rate of subsidy of Rs. 1333. The scheme covers landless labourers, small and marginal farmers, rural artisans and other workers like fishermen. Efforts have been made under this programme to select households headed by women beneficiaries. This approach will be continued during the Seventh Plan, and importance would be given to achieve a larger coverage of women.

Households headed by women would account for at least 20 per cent of the coverage. The schemes of DWCRA would be strengthened and modified in order to ensure that the benefits reach the target groups.

The National Rural Employment Programme (NREP) and Rural Landless Employment Guarantee Scheme (RLEGP) would generate additional employment in rural areas during the lean season. Stress would be laid on giving adequate employment to women beneficiaries under these schemes.

Under the programme of TRYSEM, 40 youths in the age-group, 18-35 years per development block are identified and provided training in avocations which may enable them to set up self-employment ventures. About one-third of the beneficiaries under this programme are expected to be women.

(iii) *Land reforms:* The scheme for providing financial assistance to the Assignees of Ceiling Surplus Land (ACSL) obtained from the implementation of land ceiling laws is under operation since August, 1975. The Central assistance for this scheme is intended to enable allottees to buy inputs and other necessary wherewithals of cultivation. This policy will be oriented to confer benefits on a larger number of households headed by women. Families of landless agricultural and other sections of the vulnerable groups will be given usufruct rights to grow trees on road sides, waste lands, etc.

(iv) *Industry:* Public sector undertakings would be persuaded to sponsor ancillary industries in collaboration with State level agencies dealing with development programmes for women to provide increased employment opportunities around them. Attempts would also be made to identify and target the women beneficiaries under Entrepreneurial Development Programme (EDP) and Industrial Estates.

(v) *Village and small-scale industries:* The schemes for the introduction of new technologies and the induction of expertise through upgradation of training would be further expanded. The scope of the specific training programmes for women entrepreneurs will be widened in order to fully familiarise them with the technical know-how needed for setting up enterprises. The number of such women entrepreneurs would also be increased. Rural technology institutions, and mobile technology and training units would be considerably expanded. These organisations would regularly conduct special training courses for women at various levels. The training would be oriented, wherever possible, to schemes like IRDP, TRYSEM, etc. Taking up special programmes for women by agencies like process-cum-product development centres (PPDCs), training centres and small industries services institutes (SISI) would be examined. A massive programme for training of artisans, managers, supervisors and entrepreneurs would have to be taken up to expand efficient production and for promotion of skilled employment. Women's participation in these schemes will be increased substantially.

Besides the District Industries centres (DICs) will play a special role in the identification of groups of women artisans/workers for disseminating information relating to avocations to be taken up and the nature of support that could be extended by governmental agencies.

Presently, some special provisions in terms of infrastructure facilities like industrial sheds are being extended to women entrepreneurs. As this facility is not adequate efforts would be made to set up mini-industrial estates exclusively for women on a much larger scale. Special facilities like sheds and plots at subsidised rates to units exclusively run by women and/or employing female labour will be given.

The National Small Industries Corporation and other apex organisations would extend support for marketing, product design and financial support for raw material procurement. Concessional financial requirements will also be considered for meeting fully the working capital requirements and for providing margin money for seed capital. The distinct and unique role assigned to the handloom sector will be preserved and several measures would be initiated both for consolidation and expansion of this sector.

Under the programme of training of workers and entrepreneurs, women beneficiaries will be given importance. Women are expected to obtain sizeable employment under this sector. Coir making, sericulture and small-scale industries are some such sectors which offer great potential.

(vi) *Khadi and village industries:* During the Seventh Plan the employment coverage under khadi and village industries is likely to increase from the present 3.80 million persons to 5.86 million persons. A considerable proportion of this additional employment will come to women and the percentage share of women is expected to increase from 46 to 48 per cent during the Seventh Plan.

(vii) *Other measures:* Efforts will be made towards creation and promotion of equal employment opportunities for men and women. Implementation of the Equal Remuneration Act will be strengthened to ensure that women workers are paid wages as prescribed in the Act from time to time. Studies would be sponsored to examine whether equal remuneration under the Act is related to work outputs under different sectors of employment. Similarly studies will be undertaken on the implementation of the Factories' Act 1948, the Plantation Labour Act 1951 and the Mines' Act of 1952 to assess whether the interests of women are adequately protected. Areas/sectors where women's employment is low would be identified and measures for improving their prospects will be taken. Emphasis will also be placed on the study and identification of factors that hinder women's employment. Special agencies will be set up for extending credit facilities for self-employment and home-based workers. Relaxation of age limit for women for entry into government services and public sector undertakings will be considered. Avenues for creation of part-time employment for women will also be explored.

Science and technology: Programme on 'Science and Technology for Women' would be further strengthened to identify, formulate, sponsor and implement research and development, demonstration and extension programmes, with special emphasis on providing opportunities for gainful employment, self-employment to women specially to those in rural areas.

The training programmes at different levels such as those for unemployed graduates, school drop outs and housewives will be strengthened and expanded, for improving the trainees' skills. Besides, skill manuals and training aids in areas of agriculture, animal husbandry and other new occupations would be prepared to provide opportunities of independent employment and income for women. Assistance of voluntary organisations would be sought for taking need based technologies to the target groups and in obtaining feedback regarding the acceptance of the programme and in the identification of factors that influence the transfer of technologies. Under the concept of Vigyan Kendras, the possibility of setting up rural banks for lending improved agricultural tools would be explored and new groups would be identified, preferably those in which scientists and technologists are actively involved for taking up developmental programmes for women at grass-root level.

Special training programmes would continue to be sponsored for women in polytechnics and other institutions of technical education in areas such as repair and maintenance of radios, television and other electronic hardware or consumer durables, manufacture of PVC goods, lacquer work, fibre reinforced plastics etc. Involvement of women voluntary agencies and home science colleges would be ensured.

Social Welfare: The programmes for women under the Social Welfare Sector are meant to supplement the services available to women under other developmental sectors. Further strengthening is envisaged of the ongoing schemes which have been found useful in skill formation and creation of gainful employment among women. Very close linkages with specialised agencies such as ICAR, ICMR, DST, Rural Development, Industry and Education are called for.

The Central Social Welfare Board would continue to extend grants in aid to voluntary organisations to set up a variety of income generating units under the Socio-Economic Programme' for the benefit of needy women. Efforts would be made to improve the programme by introducing better technical and marketing support. The scheme of assistance to public undertakings/corporations and autonomous organisations for supporting projects aimed at income generation and employment among women from weaker sections on a sustained basis with the help of Norwegian Agency for International Development (NORAD) would be further expanded, with focus on diversified occupations and inculcating new skills required by the job market. Grants would also be given for organising condensed educational and vocational training courses for adult women so as to improve their employment prospects. Short duration training courses (not exceeding one year) in non-traditional trades would be expanded for rehabilitating women in distress and their dependent children. Construction/ expansion of hostels for working women from low-income groups will be accelerated with a view to provide accommodation with improved standards of service at reasonable cost. The possibility of involving the inmates in the management of these hostels would be explored. The scheme of training of rural women in public cooperation will be extended to develop leadership qualities among them and to involve them in the developmental activities of the country.

A new scheme namely. Women's Development Corporations would be taken up for promoting employment generating activities by supporting schemes for women's groups and women from poorer sections of society. These corporations would identify potential areas of employment and assist beneficiaries in project formulation raising the requisite finances and marketing of their products. A Women's Development Planning and Monitoring Cell will be set up for collection of data and monitoring of Plan programmes. Provision has also been made for a few innovative schemes projects which if found successful would be replicated.

Voluntary Organisations: At present the effort by voluntary agencies is rather uneven, and is mostly concentrated in the urban areas. These agencies have to be stimulated to extend their programmes to rural hilly and backward areas. They would be encouraged to create public opinion against social evils like child marriage, dowry, illiteracy and atrocities on women. Sustained effort would be made for increasing the age at marriage of girls and for improving the adverse sex ratio. There is lack of awareness about the existing social legislation to protect the interests of women. Voluntary agencies would be supported to undertake educational work and bring in awareness among women regarding their rights and privileges. They would also be associated in extension activities.

The voluntary organisations would be involved in delivering the "Messages" on preventive and promotive health and social and nutritive care for women and children. It has been well established that blindness, leprosy, tuberculosis, polio, accidents, drug addiction and prostitution afflict vast numbers of our population. Instead of expending large sums on therapeutic and rehabilitative services (which are costly for those affected), emphasis would be on preventive care. Voluntary agencies, educational institutions and training centres would be involved and aided to take up various activities for promoting preventive measures in a planned and coordinated manner. Production of films, documentaries, literature and other forms of mass communication and deployment of non-formal channels of communication by these agencies and institutions would be fully supported. Besides, they can also take up programmes of vocational training for adult women and girls from poorer sections on a large scale in order to enlarge and improve the avenues of employment. There is an urgent need for public conveniences' for women at those bus stands, railway stations, theatres and market places which lack this amenity. Voluntary agencies would be encouraged to take up this work in a big way.

Monitoring

A proper monitoring mechanism will be developed to ensure optimal utilisation of facilities meant for women under different sectors and to minimise leakages. The special cells which are being set up in the Ministries for this purpose will be strengthened in order to ensure proper monitoring and coordination of different schemes. Steps will be taken to strengthen the machinery for monitoring progress of various schemes at State and district levels.

APPENDIX V

DEVELOPMENT OF VILLAGE LEVEL ORGANISATIONS: REPORT OF THE WORKING GROUP ON DEVELOPMENT OF VILLAGE LEVEL ORGANISATION OF RURAL WOMEN, JUNE 1987, GOVERNMENT OF INDIA, MINISTRY OF AGRICULTURE AND IRRIGATION, DEPARTMENT OF RURAL DEVELOPMENT, NEW DELHI

A Working Group was constituted by the Department of Rural Development with two-fold purposes. One of the purpose was to review the objectives and functioning of associate organisation. Mahila Mandals and Youth clubs as well as their links with other agencies. The second purpose was to make recommendations on the basis of the findings especially about programmes to be implemented through the organisation, coordination with the work of other agencies, association of weaker sections with the associate organisations, and strengthening the cadre of workers or extension agents.

For detailed deliberations three sub-groups were

constituted. These included sub-groups on the needs of rural women, objectives of Mahila Mandals and their involvement in rural development; sub-group on rural youth, their promotion, strengthening and training for participation in rural development programmes; and sub-group on block, district and state level functionaries for women's programmes and their training.

The report was submitted in two parts. Part I dealt with village level organisations for rural women including indicators of neglect, assessment of existing programme, new programmes, implications, and so forth. Part II dealt with development of rural youth organisation particularly to promote and strengthen. Yuvak Mandals.

Sixth Five-Year Plan 1980-85: Women and Development
Chapter 27—Government of India, Planning Commission, New Delhi

The Constitution of India not only provides for equal rights and privileges for women and men but also for making special provision for women. A series, of social legislations have been enacted from time to time for raising the status of women in the country. The Five-Year Plans have consistently placed special emphasis on providing minimum health facilities integrated with family welfare and nutrition for women and children, acceleration of women's education, their increase in the labour force and welfare services for women in need. Various welfare and development schemes have been introduced to improve the living conditions of women and to increase their access to and control over material and social resources. Special steps have been taken to remove legal, social and other constraints to enable them to make use of the rights and new opportunities becoming available for them.

Various studies show that women, are becoming increasingly conscious of their rights and capabilities. However, the demographic features of female population like excessive mortality in female children resulting in persistent decline in sex ratio, low rate of literacy, and low economic status stress the need for greater attention to the economic emancipation of women. The low status of women in large segments of Indian society cannot be raised without opening up of opportunities of independent employment and income for them. But the process of change to raise the status of women under various spheres of socio-economic activities would require sustained effort over a period of time.

Review

Under the different Five-Year Plans, general as well as special programmes were taken up for the welfare of women and also to cater to their special requirements. A wide network of maternity and child health centres and family welfare centres were established. An attempt to integrate the family welfare programme with general health services has been made. Prophylaxis against nutritional anaemia amongst mothers and immunisation of pregnant women against tetanus has been taken up along with prophylaxis against blindness in children caused by Vitamin 'A' deficiency and immunisation against diphtheria, whooping-cough, tetanus and polio for children.

Special nutrition programme was started in 1970-71 for providing nutritional supplements to the most vulnerable group of pregnant and nursing mothers and children of the age-group 0—5. Nutrition education has been made a basic component of supplementary nutrition, health and education programmes.

Emphasis has been laid on increasing the enrolment of girls in schools by providing various incentives. Functional literacy as part of the national adult education programme as well as under the Integrated Child Development Services projects have been given special emphasis.

The Equal Remuneration Act aims to eliminate discrimination in remuneration against women. Labour laws have been made to provide for material benefits and creches in units employing women.

Social welfare programmes cater to the special needs of women who by reason of some handicap—social, economic, physical or mental—are unable to avail of or are traditionally denied the amenities and services provided by the community. In the beginning, emphasis was on the provision of institutional services but it has now been shifted to the preventive and developmental aspects.

Despite all these development measures and the Constitutional legal guarantees, women have lagged behind men in almost all sectors. There has been a steady decline in sex ratio. For 1,000 men there were 972 women in 1901, which became 946 in 1951 and 930 in 1971, while the position is opposite in the developed countries. Sex ratio for all ages in 1971 was 951 for rural areas and 857 for urban areas. The inter-State variations are considerable. The ratio is adverse in the States of Punjab, Uttar Pradesh, Jammu and Kashmir and West Bengal. It is most favourable in Kerala, followed by Orissa, Tamil Nadu and Andhra Pradesh. Similarly, the expectation of life at birth, a good indicator of development, shows that it is 44.7 for the females against 46.4 for the males in 1971.

The surveys by the Registrar-General of India reveal that the infant mortality rate (IMR) is more among female babies as compared to males in rural and urban areas as may be seen from the table below:

Infant Mortality Rate by Sex and Residence

Year	*Rural*		*Urban*		*All India*	
	Male	*Female*	*Male*	*Female*	*Male*	*Female*
1972	141	161	85	85	132	148
1978	130	142	69	71	120	131

It has been estimated that in 1978-79 of the total non-enrolled children of the age-group 6-14, two-thirds were girls. In 1979-80, in the age-group 6-11, the population of girls in schools was two-thirds that of the boys (about 66 per cent for girls against about 100.2 per cent for boys). In the age-group 11-14, the number of girls in the schools was half that of the boys (28 per cent for girls and 52.0 per cent for boys).

In literacy also, excluding 0—4 years age-group, the number of women literates is less than half of the males (*i.e.,* 21.97 per cent for women against 45.95 per cent for males). The rural female literacy rate is only 13.2 per cent (1971) while the urban rate is 42.3 per cent. About 83 districts have less than 5 per cent female literacy and 113 between 5 and 10 per cent. The female literacy for scheduled caste is 6.44 per cent and for scheduled tribe is 4.85 per cent. The rates of literacy varied widely from 3.58 per cent in Arunachal Pradesh, 4.8 per cent in Rajasthan, 7.2 per cent in Bihar to 61 per cent in Kerala.

Despite preventive legislation, the age of marriage for girls specially in rural areas and lower strata of society has remained low. The Report of the Committee on the Status of Women shows that the percentage of girls married by 14 years of age in rural areas in 1961 was as high as 22 as compared to 7 among the urban females of the same age-group. By 1971, this percentage came down to 14 in rural areas while it dropped to 4 in urban areas. Early marriages result in frequent pregnancies, poor health and lack of opportunity for proper personality development. Repeated pregnancies account for high incidence of anaemia and maternal malnutrition, ultimately leading to high maternal mortality rate.

Women labour force participation rate remained generally unchanged for the last three decades around 28 per cent while in the case of men it was fairly stable around 57 per cent. In the orgnaised sector the women's share increased only slightly form 11 per cent in 1971 to 12.4 per cent in 1979. A few women in all walks of life reached the top positions but on the whole they continue to be concentrated mainly in low-scale, low-wage and drudgery involving jobs. Women are mainly employed in the unorganised sector which forms the overwhelming majority of female workers (over 90 per cent). This is also linked with their low rate of participation in the training programmes in industrial training institutes, polytechnics, engineering colleges, Krishi Vigyan Kendras, technical and industrial schools, though special measures to expand training opportunities for women in non-traditional occupations have been taken. The details given in Annexures 27.1 and 27.2 are relevant in this regard.

Strategy

The main drawbacks in women's development have thus been mainly preoccupation with repeated pregnancies without respite in physical workload, lack of education—formal and non-formal and a preponderance of social prejudices along with lack of independent economic generation activity or independent assets. The strategy thus has to be threefold—of education employment and health. They are interdependent and dependent on the total developmental process. In addition, the voluntary adoption of the small family norm has to be promoted among all couples.

In the Plan, the basic approach is of the family as a unit of development. Within this approach, special attention on the most vulnerable members will be given. The most vulnerable members may change from family to family and within the family from time to time. But for some time in future, women will continue to be one of the most vulnerable members of the family. Hence, the economic emancipation of the family with specific attention to women education of children and family planning will constitute the three major operational aspects of the family centred poverty alleviation strategy.

In order to understand and analyse the backwardness of women a disaggregated view of the problem, according to groups, communities and areas is necessary. An aggregate picture is sometimes misleading, e.g., the average female literacy in India is 22 per cent against about 4 per cent in Arunachal Pradesh.

Separate cells in organisations and agencies generating substantial employment opportunities to look after the women's interests are helpful but have a limited role. It is more important to create a general awareness' and understanding of the problems of women's employment in all the top policy and decision-making and executive personnel. There is also the special problem facing women like the preference for male children for social and cultural reasons. This will require awareness, understanding and action. The best way to do so is to educate the children, orient the teachers, examine the text books and teaching-aids and ensure that the next generation grows up with new thinking. As it is not enough to wait for them, non-formal education of men and women is necessary as an immediate short-term measure. Both men and women need education in home science so that the concept of symmetrical families can take root.

In order to take corrective measures as the programmes are implemented, the statistical data of physical achievement in beneficiary-oriented programmes will have to be collected by sex. The implementation of programmes would be reviewed from time to time.

Economic independence would accelerate the improvement of the status of women. Government would endeavour to give joint titles to husband and wife in all development activities involving transfer of assets. This would be taken up for implementation to start within programmes like distribution of land and house-sites and beneficiary-oriented economic units.

Voluntary action has a key role to play in mobilising public support against social prejudices. Hence its strengthening at the grassroot level will be necessary. Such organisation of voluntary action is necessary for creating a proper climate for the introduction of social legislation as well as for its effective implementation and the provision of legal aid.

For promoting adequate developmental efforts for women at different levels and creating needed channels for women to participate effectively in decisions that affect their lives, grass root level organisations should be promoted. Mahila Mandals and other voluntary agencies would be encouraged to take up socio-economic programmes for providing wages and self-employment in rural areas. They would be linked with cooperatives and federations for marketing of products. Adequate attention should be paid to offer technical and managerial assistance to these agencies so that they would prepare viable economic projects for attracting institutional finance and market their products. Marketing, being crucial to the programme, the arrangements would need to be reviewed.

The Central Social Welfare Board would continue to be largely responsible to extend support, both technical and financial, to voluntary agencies, particularly in the backward areas. The programmes of the Central Social Welfare Board and those of individual developments will be functionally integrated so as to optimise the benefits from all programmes intended for women.

Advisory Committees at different levels would be set up for reviewing the adequacy of the implementing machineries and periodic progress for various social legislations such as Anti-Dowry Act, Child Marriage Restraint Act, Indian Succession Act, etc. The National Committee for Women headed by the Prime Minister will provide overall guidance and leadership in this field.

At district levels, special cell for increasing women's participation through wage and self-employment would be set up as part of the proposed machinery for district manpower planning and employment generation.

Research and studies to imporve data base regarding women would be supported. Coordination, evaluation and monitoring of the programmes would need to be improved. Science and technology to reduce drudgery of household work would be supported.

Education

The programmes for universalisation of elementary education will be specially directed towards higher enrolment and retention of girls in schools. This would require Balwari-cum-creches attached to the schools to enable the girls to attend school since otherwise they would have to stay at home to look after the younger brothers and sisters in the absence of mothers at work. It would also require income-generation work for girls outside the schools hours to supplement to family's income. Other incentives like uniforms, free books and stationery etc., already in force, would need to be effectively expanded. Women teachers, where necessary, would be appointed in rural areas to encourage girls education. Residential quarters for women teachers would also be constructed. Science teaching in girls' schools/colleges will be strengthened to achieve greater participation of women in science and technology. Admission policies will be streamlined to promote greater enrolment of women in engineering, electronics, agricultural, veterinary, fishery and forestry courses. In education and training, women would thus be brought to the mainstream along with men to share the facilities fully.

The functional literacy programme would be expanded, specially in areas having low female literacy rates. Special non-formal educational programmes will be introduced for girls in the age-group 15-20 years who could not complete formal schooling earlier. Every effort will be made to ensure that at-least 1/3 of trainees under the TRYSEM programme are girls. Special Krishi, Udyog and Van Vigyan Kendras will be established for women.

For boosting the programmes for education of women belonging to backward classes the number of girls' hostels would be increased. The rates of post-matric scholarships for different courses are higher for girls as compared to boys. This scheme would be further expanded to provide larger opportunities for girls. Instead of increasing separate women's polytechnics, which were developed as multipurpose institutions for imparting training in arts, crafts, etc., co-educational institutions would be encouraged as far as possible.

Health

In health, provision will be made for continuing and expanding the maternal and child health schemes including anti-natal, natal and post-natal services, training of popular 'DAIS' who are already practising in every village so as to reduce the maternal and neo-natal deaths and complications. Training capacity of ANMs would be further augmented to meet the requirement of sub-centres. Experience reveals that ANMs posted in rural areas are not able to adjust to the local conditions due to lack of familiarity with the socio-cultural situation, accommodation and security. To overcome these field problems, efforts would be made to select girls from local areas, relax minimum educational qualifications, raise upper-age limit and give preference to widows or deserted women. In almost all the hospitals, the nursing personnel are mainly female. The training facilities for them will be expanded. Family welfare programmes will receive high priority. Sustained efforts would be made to create consciousness, acceptance and demand for this programme. Co-operation of the voluntary organisations would be sought for disseminating relevant health and family planning information and for launching a national movement for population stabilisation.

Effort would be made to expand the minimum health facilities integrated with family welfare and nutrition. The nutritional status of a child at birth is influenced by the nutritional status of his mother. It is well documented that a vast majority of pregnant and nursing mothers, especially belonging to the low socio-economic group, live on diets which are inadequate. The high incidence of prematurity, low birth weight of babies and neo-natal mortality can be attributed to poor nutritional condition among the mothers. In view of this, importance will be given to improving the maternal nutrition status. With an increase in women's employment, the income of the household would go up thereby resulting not only in raising the nutrition and child-care in the family but also bringing down the birth rate and infant mortality rate.

The long-term approach to solving the problem of malnutrition in women would be to generate employment among them as it would provide purchasing power to women which will have an impact on her as well as her family's nutritional status. Along with this, basic services like health creche-cum-balwadis, etc., would be provided to enable their employment retention. Till the long-term programme effectively builds up, nutrition intervention to most vulnerable groups of women, namely pregnant and nursing mothers from the weakest sections of the society, would continue to get nutrition supplement under the supplementary Nutrition Programme. Education will also be imparted on the production and consumption of nutritious foods and on the adoption of simple horticultural remedies involving kitchen gardening for the major nutritional maladies of each block.

Employment

One of the most important means of achieving improvement in the status of women would be to secure for them a fair share of employment opportunities. Areas and sectors where women's employment is either low or on the decline would be identified and corrective measures initiated to promote additional avenues for employment. Efforts would be made to offer larger employment for in the schemes for public distribution system, rural godowns, Operation Flood II, Dairy Development and social forestry and in armed forces. Modernisation of traditional occupations of women such as spinning and weaving, match-making, coir, cashew, rural marketing, agriculture, animal husbandary and fishery, etc., would be selective and would include simultaneous development of skills for alternative employment for them. Mechanisation will be encouraged in such areas where the processing or manufacturing involves extremely strenuous and debilitating hard work which is injurious to health. The impact of new projects on women's employment will be monitored.

Family aid services would be supported so as to enable women to remain in employment. Enforcement of statutory obligations for setting up creches would be pursued vigorously. Creches would be established in the hostels for working women. State and Central Government offices, public sector undertakings, residential colonies and projects sites. Creches will have to be designed for regular establishments as well as for agricultural, construction and migrant labour families. In rural areas this would be linked up with the scheme of NREP. The implementation of the Equal Remuneration Act would be reviewed and appropriate measures introduced for their effective functioning. Measures would be taken for the payment of wages/salaries earned by women directly to them.

The specific needs and problems of self-employed women will be identified and steps taken to extend appropriate support to self-employed women like street vendors, petty shop-keepers, weavers, etc.

A major step to be taken to promote female employment would be to expand and diversify the education and training opportunities available to women. Bias is often at work to prevent women from joining certain types of education and training in sufficient numbers. Appropriate training facilities would be initiated for the skill-development of women job seekers to promote their employability including self-employment. They would be eligible for employment and training in all fields provided they fulfil the required qualifications. Under the Apprenticeship Training Scheme, placement of increased number of women trainees would receive special attention. Under the vocational training Programme for women, rural training component and setting up of more regional institutions are envisaged. The national scheme of Training of Rural Youth for Self-Employment (TRYSEM) is expected to cover a large number of rural women. These would also be expected to facilitate the removal of skill constraints and biases working against the recruitment of women trainees. A fair share of stipends, hostel seats, etc. would be made available in order to facilitate rapid growth in the number of female trainees. As an incentive, special prizes and awards may be instituted for women trainees or students in recognised institutes. The programmes would be integrated with production activities.

Social Welfare

The coverage of the programme of hostels for working women would be stepped up with emphasis on making this scheme a self-financing project as far as possible. Measures for re-entry of women who go out of employment for raising heir families would be considered along with the provision of part-time jobs in an organised manner. Besides arrangements for keeping their knowledge up-to-date, specially in science and technology would be considered. Training and rehabilitation schemes for women in need of care and protection would be formulated to facilitate their absorption into the normal stream of socio-economic life. Institutional services would be expanded selectively to provide shelter to the most needy and unrehabilitable category only. The socially and physically handicapped women would be helped to take advantage of the services provided under social defence and handicapped sub-sectors of social welfare programmes. However, the trades under the training programmes under various institutions would have to be diversified to make their rehabilitation successful.

In summary, the major thrust of the VI Plan in the field of welfare of women is their economic upliftment through greater opportunities for salaried, self and wage employment. For this purpose appropriate technologies, services and public policies will be introduced. The technological package will include imparting new skills and upgrarding existing skills. The services package will pay attention to training and credit needs and to marketing. The public policy package will include measures in the area of ownership rights, enforcement of wage laws and employment of women in development projects. Women's organisations will be assisted to grow in effectiveness. Specific attention will be paid for the removal of socio-economic biases resulting in the neglect of female children and women. Measures for their improvement of health and nutritional status will be strengthened. Programmes relating to education, health, nutrition and employment would no doubt go a long way in the removal of social disabilities facing women. However, the improvements in the socio-economic status of women would depend to a large extent on the social change in the value system, attitudes and social structure prevailing in the country.

Bibliography

Adisa, Opal Palmer (1992).Undeclared war: African-American women writers explicating rape.*Women's Studies International Forum* v15, n3 (May-June, 1992):363

Adjetey, Fitnat Naa-Adjeley (1995). Reclaiming the African Woman's Individuality: The Struggle Between Women's Reproductive Autonomy and African Society and Culture. *American University Law Review,* 44, 1351.

Ahmad, L. (1989). Arab Culture and Writing Women's Bodies. *Feminist Issues,* Spring:41-55.

Ahuja, Ram (1986). *Crime Against Women,* Jaipur: Rawat Publishers.

Asia Watch and Human Rights Watch (1993). *A Modern Form of Slavery: Trafficking of Burmese Women and Girls into Brothels in Thailand.* Human Rights Watch, NY.

Bandura, A. (1973). *Aggression: A Social Learning Analysis,* Englewood Cliffs: Prentice Hall.

Bonnerjea, Lucy (1985). Shaming the world: the needs of women refugees. London: CHANGE.

Bowker, L.H. (1981). "Wife beating" in Women and Crime in America, New York: Macmillan.

Boyd, Monica (1994) Canada's refugee flows: gender

inequality. (more men than women admitted to Canada as refugees) *Canadian Social Trends,* n32 (Spring, 1994):7 (4 pages).

Boyd, Monica. Canada's refugee flows: gender inequality. (more men than women admitted to Canada as refugees) *Canadian Social Trends,* n32 (Spring, 1994):7 (4 pages).

Brownmiller, Susan (1975). *Against Our Will: Women and Rape.*

Bunch, Charlotte (1995). Beijing, Backlash, and the Future of Women's Human Rights. *Health and Human Rights,* 1(4):449.

Bunch, Charlotte (1995). The Global Campaign for Women's Human Rights: Where Next After Vienna? *St. John's Law Review,* 69(1-2):171-178.

Bunting, Annie (1993). Theorizing Women's Cultural Diversity in Feminist International Human Rights Strategies. *Journal of Law and Society*, 20(1):6-22.

Card, Claudia.(1996). Rape as a weapon of war.(Special Issue: Women and Violence) *Hypatia* v11, n4 (Fall, 1996):5 (14 pages).

Center for Women's Global Citizenship, (1994). *Gender Violence and Women's Human Rights in Africa.,* Women, Ink.

Charter, Winston (1987). The Rights of Women, the African Charter, and the Economic Development of Africa. *Boston College Third World Law Journal,* 7:215.

Chhabra, K.S. (1982). 'Woman and the Law', *Law Journal of the Guru Nanak Dev University,* Vol. 10, No. 1.

Chinkin, Christine (1993). The Hunger Trap: Women, Food, and Self-Determination. *Michigan Journal of International Law,* 262(1993).

Chinkin,Christine (1995).Violence against Women: The International Legal Response. *Gender-and-Development;* 1995, 3, 2, June, 23-28.

Cipriani, Linda (1993). "Gender and Persecution" Protecting Women Under International Law. *Georgia Immigration Law Journal,* 7,511.

Clark, Belinda (1991). The Vienna Convention reservations regime and the Convention on Discrimination against Women. *American Journal of International Law* v85, n2 (April, 1991):281-321.

Cook, Rebecca (1994). *Human Rights of Women. National and International Perspectives.* University of Pennsylvania Press, Philadelphia.

Cook, Rebecca (1994). *Women's Health and Human Rights: The Promotion and Protection of Women's Health Through International Human Rights Law.*

Cook, Rebecca (1995). International Human Rights and Women's Reproductive Health. *Studies in Family Planning,* 24,73.

Copelon, Rhonda (1994). Surfacing Gender: Re-engravingCrimes Against Women in Humanitarian Law. *Hastings Women's Law Journal,* 5,243.

Copelon, Rhonda (1995). Women and War Crimes. *St. John's Law Review,* 69(1-2):61-68.

Dallmeyer, Dorinda ed (1993). *Reconceiving Reality: Women and International Law.*

Davidson, Miriam (1994). Second-class refugees: persecuted women are denied asylum. (Cover Story) *Progressive* v58, n6 (June, 1994):22 (4 pages).

Dixon-Mueller, Ruth (1993). *Population Policies and Women's Rights: Transforming Reproductive Choice.* Praeger, Westport:CN.

Drinan, Robert F.(1988).World law protects the rights of women. *America* v159, n4 (Aug 6, 1988):87 (3 pages).

Dyches, Hayne and Beth Rushing (1993). The Health Status of Women in the World- System. *International Journal of Health Services,* 23(2):359-371.

Ekachai, Sanitsuda (1993). Women, war and violence. *off our backs* v23, n4 (April, 1993):7.

El Saadawi, N. (1980). *The Hidden Face of Eve: Women in the Arab World.* Zed Press, London.

Elder, Betty-G. (1986).The Rights of Women: Their Status in International Law. *Crime-and-Social-Justice;* 1986, 25, 1-39.

Epp, Marlene (1997). The memory of violence: Soviet and East European Mennonite refugees and rape on the second World War. *Journal of Women's History* v9, n1 (Spring, 1997):58 (30 pages).

Etienne, Margareth (1995). Addressing Gender-Based Violence in an International Context. *Harvard Women's Law Journal,* 18:139.

FitzGerald, Anne (1992).The secret torture. (custodial rape of women) *New Statesman & Society* v5, n213 (July 31, 1992):21

Gellner, Myriam (1989). Sexual violence against women refugees: from private sorrows to international politics.

Giffen, K (1994). Women's health and the privatization of fertility control in Brazil. *Social Science and Medicine,* 39(3):355-60.

Gilbert, Lauren (1995). Rights, Refugee Women & Reproductive Health. *American University Law Review,* 44, 1213.

Gillespie, Marcia Ann (1992). No woman's land. (women refugees) *Ms. Magazine* v3, n3 (Nov-Dec, 1992):18 (5 pages)..

Ginzburg, Faye (1991). What do Women Want?: Feminist Anthropology Confronts Clitoridectomy. *Medical Anthropology Quarterly,* 5(1):17-19.

Gomez, Elsa Gomez (1993). *Gender, Women and Health in the Americas.* PAHO, Washington, DC.

Goode, W.J. (1974). "Force and Violence in the Family," in Steinmetz and Strauss (ed.), *Violence in the Family,* New York: Harper and Row.

Heise, Lori L.(1993). Reproductive freedom and violence against women: where are the intersections? *Journal of Law, Medicine & Ethics* v21, n2 (Summer, 1993):206-216.

Hicks, George (1995).*The comfort women.* St Leonards, NSW : Allen & Unwin,1995.

Keely, Charles B. The resettlement of women and children refugees. (Features) *Migration World Magazine* v20, n4 (Sept-Oct, 1992):14 (5 pages).

Keely, Charles B.(1992). The resettlement of women and children refugees. (Features) *Migration World Magazine* v20, n4 (Sept-Oct, 1992):14 (5 pages).

Kelly, Nancy (1993). Double standard. (how laws and regulations defining refugees are constructed by men) *Women's Review of Books* v10, n10-11 (July, 1993):17 (2 pages).

Kelly, Nancy (1993). Gender Related Persecution: Assessing the Asylum Claims of Women. *Cornell International Law Journal,* 625-633.

Kohn, E A. (1994). Rape as a Weapon of War: Women's

Human Rights During the Dissolution of Yugoslavia. *Golden Gate University Law Review,* 24(199).

Koss, May; Paul Koss, and Joy Woodruff (1991). Deleterious Effects of Criminal Victimization on Women's Health and Medical Utilization. *Archives of Internal Medicine,* 151:342.

Larson, Lori Ann (1996). Female Genital Mutilation In the United States: Child Abuse or Constitutional Freedom? *Women's Rights Law Reporter,* 17(2):237.

Martin, D. (1979). "What keeps a woman captive in a violent relationship," in Moore, D.M. (ed.) *Battered Women,* Beverly Hills: Sage Publications.

Neuwirth, Gertrud and Christine Vincent, eds. (1997).Women refugees in international perspectives, 1980-1990: an annotated bibliography. Research Resource Division for Refugees, 1997.

Russell, Ruth V.; Stage, Frances K.(1996). Leisure as burden: Sudanese refugee women. *Journal of Leisure Research* v28, n2 (Spring, 1996):108 (14 pages).

Saporta Sternbach, Nancy (1991). Re-membering the Dead: Latin American Women's "Testimonial" Discourse. *Latin American Perspectives,* 70(18:3):91-102.

Shepherd, Judith (1992). Post-traumatic stress disorder in Vietnamese women. (Refugee Women andTheir Mental Health: Shattered Societies, Shattered Lives, part 2).*Women & Therapy* v13, n3 (Sept-Oct, 1992):281 (16 pages).

Stairs, Felicite & Lori Pope (1990). No Place Like Home: Assaulted Migrant Women's Claims to Refugee Status. *Journal of Law and Social Policy,* 148.

Sullivan, Donna (1994). Women's Human Rights and the

1993 World Conference on Human Rights. *American University Journal of International Law and Policy,* 152.

Swiss, Shana; Nowrojee, Binaifer. Women are the silent victims in Liberia. (Forum: ViewPoint). *Africa News* v37, n5 (Nov 23, 1992):5.

Tamale, Sylvia (1992). Rape Law and the Violation of Women in Uganda: A Critical Perspective. *Uganda Law Society Review,* 195-215.

Thomas, Dorothy (1995). Women's Human Rights: From Visibility to Accountability. *St. John's Law Review,* 69(1-2):217-230.

Tierney, Kathleen (1994). The Evolution of Women's Asylums Since 1500: From Refugees for Ex-Prostitutes to Shelters for Battered Women. (book reviews) *Contemporary Sociology* v23, n4 (July, 1994):581 (2 pages).

Tinklenberg, J.R. (1973). "Alcohol and Violence," in Bourne and Fox (eds.), *Alcoholism Progress in Research and Treatment,* New York: Academic Press.

Toubia, Nahid (1988). Women and Health in Sudan. In *Women of the Arab World.* Toubia, N. ed. Zed Books, London.

Turshen, Meredith ed. (1991). *Women and Health in Africa.* Africa World Press, Inc. Trenton, NJ.

Wali, Sima (1994). Repatriation and the reconstruction of Afghanistan: the role of women. *Migration World Magazine* v22, n4 (Sept-Oct, 1994):26 (3 pages).

Wali, Sima (1995). Human Rights for Refugee and Displaced Women. In Peters and Wolper, eds. Women's Rights, Human Rights.

Wali, Sima. Repatriation and the reconstruction of Afghanistan: the role of women. *Migration World Magazine* v22, n4 (Sept-Oct, 1994):26 (3 pages).

Walker, Alice and Pratibha Parmar (1993).*Warrior Marks. Female Genital Mutilation and the Sexual Blinding of Women.* Harcourt Brace and Co., NY.

Walker, L. (1979). *The Battered Women,* New York: Harper and Row.

Ward, Martha (1993). A Different Disease: HIV/AIDS and Health Care for Women in Poverty. *Culture, Medicine and Psychiatry,* 17(4):414.

Wheeler, David L.(1996). Harvard programme helps change the law. (Women Refugees Project) *Chronicle of Higher Education* v42, n43 (July 5, 1996):A5.

Winter, Bronwyn (1994). Women, the Law, and Cultural Relativism in France: The Case of Excision. *Signs,* 19(4):939.

Wolfgang, M.E. (1978). "Violence in the Family," in Kutash *et al. Perspectives in Murder and Aggression,* San Francisco.

Women refugees: the caretakers adrift. *UN Chronicle* v28, n3 (Sept, 1991):51 (2 pages).

Index

W